THE "LIVING CONSTITUTION" AND THE RIGHT TO DIE

HENRY MARK HOLZER

Bestseller Amazon Author

THE "LIVING CONSTITUTION" AND THE RIGHT TO DIE
Henry Mark Holzer

Copyright © 2022 Henry Mark Holzer. All rights reserved.

A Madison Press Book
Paradise Hills, New Mexico

No part of this book may be reproduced, scanned, or distributed in any printed or electronic form without permission. Please do not participate in or encourage piracy of copyrighted materials in violation of the author's rights.

This book was proudly printed in the United States of America.

www.henrymarkholzer.com
www.henrymarkholzer.blogspot.com
hank@henrymarkholzer.com

In Memoriam

*To the countless conscripted Americans
who died in our Nation's wars*

In *Arver v. United States* (*Selective Draft Law Cases*), 245 U.S. 366 (1918), the Supreme Court of the United States upheld the constitutionality of World War I's draft law, citing with approval *The Law of Nations*, by eighteenth-century Swiss scholar-diplomat Emmerich de Vattel. According to him,

> every citizen is *bound to serve and defend the State* as far as he is able. *Society* cannot otherwise be preserved; and this union for the common defense is one of the first objects of all political association. Whoever is able to bear arms must take them up as soon as he is *ordered* to do so by the one who has the power to make war... . Since every citizen or subject is *obliged to serve the State*, the sovereign has the right, when the necessity arises, *to conscript whom he pleases*. [My emphasis.]

In other words, some people can be preserved only by forcing other people to preserve them, even at the cost of those people's lives.

Conscription is another fatal example of the consequences of altruism, collectivism, and statism in the American political, social, judicial, and constitutional systems. Countless conscripted Americans died in the Civil War, World War I, World War II, Korea, and Vietnam.

The draftees died not merely from powder and steel, but also from the immoral belief that, depending on the circumstances, Americans are no more than sacrificial animals, enslaved to the needs and wants of the state. The pandemic of 2020-2021 is another example.

Thus, the corollary question: If Americans have no right to live, do we have the moral or constitutional right to die on our own terms, when, where, why, and how we choose?

If not, why not?

To Lance Gotko, Esq.

TABLE OF CONTENTS

Table of Cases ix

Preface xiii

1. Introduction 1
2. Definitions 3
3. Historical Context 7
4. Magna Carta; Fourteenth Amendment; Procedural Due Process 9
5. "Substantive" Due Process 17
6. "Incorporation" of the Fourteenth Amendment 35
7. *Poe* v. *Ullman*: Birth of *Griswold* v. *Connecticut* 53
8. *Griswold* v. *Connecticut*: Prelude to *Roe* v. *Wade* 55
9. *Roe* v. *Wade*: Overture to *Compassion in Dying* v. *Washington* 67
10. *Compassion in Dying* v. *Washington*; Federal District Court 77
11. *Compassion in Dying* v. *Washington*; Federal Circuit Court 83

12. *Compassion in Dying* v. *Washington*;
Federal Circuit Court, *en banc* ... 87

13. Washington v. Glucksberg: Supreme Court
of the United States ... 91

14. Ninth Amendment and Unenumerated Rights ... 97

15. Conclusion ... 105

Endnotes ... 107

Appendix A ... 113

Appendix B ... 115

Other Books By Henry Mark Holzer ... 123

Acknowledgments ... 125

Henry Mark Holzer ... 126

TABLE OF CASES

Arver v. United States (Selective Draft Law Cases), 245 U.S. 366 (1918)

Barron v. Baltimore, 7 Pet. 243 (1833)

Benton v. Maryland, 395 U.S. 784 (1969)

Buck v. Bell, 274 U.S. 200 (1927)

Chicago, Milwaukee & St. Paul Railway Company v. Minnesota, 134 U.S. 418 (1890)

Compassion in Dying v. Washington; federal district court; 850 F.Supp. 1454 (USDC WD Wash) (1994)

Compassion in Dying v. Washington; federal circuit court; 49 F.3d 586 (9th Cir) (1995)

Compassion in Dying v. Washington; federal circuit court, *en banc*; 79 F.3d 790 (9th Cir) (1996)

Corfield v. Coryell, 6 F. Cas. 546 (1823)

Davidson v. New Orleans, 96 U.S. 97 (1878)

Dred Scot v. Sandford, 60 U.S. (19 How.) 393 (1857)

Gitlow v. New York, 268 U.S. 652 (1925)

Griswold v. *Connecticut*, 381 U.S. 479 (1965)

Jones v. *Flowers*, 547 U.S. 220 (2006)

Maher v. *Roe*, 432 U.S. 464 (1977)

Monongahela Navigation Co. v. *United States*, 148 U.S. 312 (1893)

Mugler v. *Kansas*, 123 U.S. 623 (1887)

Muller v. *Oregon*, 218 U.S. 412 (1980)

Palko v. *Connecticut*, 302 U.S. 319 (1937)

Planned Parenthood v. *Casey*, 505 U.S. 833 (1992)

Poe v. *Ullman*, 367 U.S. 497 (1956)

Roe v. *Wade*, 410 U.S. 113 (1973)

Schenck v. *United States*, 249 U.S. 47 (1919)

Skinner v. *Oklahoma*, 316 U.S. 535 (1942)

Smyth v. *Ames*, 171 U.S. 362 (1898)

Timbs v. *Indiana*, 586 U.S.___, 139 S.Ct. 682 (2019)

Vanhorne's Lessee v. *Dorance*, 2 U.S. (2 Dall.) 304 (1795)

Washington v. *Glucksberg*, 571 U.S. 702 (1997)

Wynehamer v. *The People of the State of New York*, 13 N.Y. 378 (1856)

OTHER RESOURCES

44 *Brooklyn Law Review* 725 (1978)

106 *Mich. L. Rev.* 1501 (2008)

Declaration of Independence

Hon. Robert J. Bork, United States Court of Appeals, District of Columbia Circuit

The American Constitution and Ayn Rand's "Inner Contradiction"

Webster's New World Dictionary of the American Language

PREFACE

The callous remark of Justice O.W. Holmes, Jr.— "Three generations of imbeciles are enough."— was made in his less than three-page majority (8–1) opinion in the 1927 United States Supreme Court case of *Carrie Buck v. Bell, Superintendent of the State Colony for Epileptics and Feeble Minded.*

Holmes's opinion endorsing the State of Virginia's compulsory sterilization of Carrie Buck pursuant to Virginia's law bears heavily on the related thesis of this book: *Americans' lives are owned not by ourselves but instead by the "government" (often called "society"), and thus we do not possess the correlated right to die when, where, why, and how we choose.*

Immediately below, are the relevant parts of Holmes's opinion for the Court. [The italics, ellipses, and bracketed words are mine.]

> Mr. Justice HOLMES delivered the opinion of the Court.
>
> [T]he superintendent of the State Colony for Epileptics and Feeble Minded, was ordered to perform the operation of salpingectomy upon Carrie Buck ... for the purpose of making her sterile. The case comes here upon the contention that the statute ... is void under the Fourteenth

Amendment as denying to the plaintiff ... due process of law and the equal protection of the laws.

Carrie Buck is a feeble-minded white woman who was committed to the State Colony.... She is the daughter of a feeble-minded mother in the same institution, and the mother of an illegitimate feeble-minded child. She was eighteen years old at the time of the trial of her case .... An Act of Virginia ... recites that the health of the patient and *the welfare of society may be promoted* in certain cases by the sterilization of mental defectives, under careful safeguard, etc.; that the sterilization may be effected in males by vasectomy and in females by salpingectomy, without serious pain or substantial danger to life; that the Commonwealth is supporting in various institutions many defective persons who if now discharged would *become a menace* but if incapable of procreating might be discharged with safety and become self-supporting with benefit to themselves *and to society*; and that experience has shown that *heredity plays an important part in the transmission of insanity, imbecility, etc.* The statute then enacts that whenever the superintendent of certain institutions including the abovenamed State Colony shall be of opinion that it is for the best interest of the patients *and of society* that an inmate under his care should be sexually sterilized, he may have the operation performed upon any patient afflicted with hereditary forms of insanity, imbecility, etc., on complying with the very careful provisions by which the act protects the patients from possible abuse. [My emphasis.]

[A]ny party may apply to the [Virginia] Supreme Court of Appeals, which, if it grants the appeal, is to hear the case upon the record of the trial in the Circuit Court and may enter such order as it thinks the Circuit Court should have entered. There can be no doubt that so far as procedure is concerned the rights of the patient are most carefully considered, and as every step in this case was taken in scrupulous compliance with the statute and after months of observation, there is no doubt that in that respect the plaintiff in error has had due process at law.

Please note the following sentence's dichotomy between *procedu[ral]* and *substantive* law, which, as we shall see, play a crucial role in why Americans have no constitutional right to die.

> The [plaintiff's] attack is not upon the [statute's] *procedure* but upon the *substantive law*. It seems to be contended that in no circumstances could such an order be justified. It certainly is contended that the order cannot be justified upon the existing grounds. The judgment [of the Virginia court] finds the facts that have been recited and that Carrie Buck "is the *probable* potential parent of *socially inadequate* offspring, likewise afflicted, that she may be sexually sterilized without detriment to her general health and that her welfare *and that of society* will be promoted by her sterilization," and thereupon makes the order. In view of the general declarations of the Legislature and the specific findings of the Court obviously we cannot say ... that the grounds do not exist, and if they exist they justify the result. *We have seen more than once that the public welfare may call upon the best citizens for their lives* [see *In Memoriam* and *Selective Draft Law Cases*, above. [Emphasis and bracketed words are mine.]

> It would be strange if it [the public welfare] could not call upon *those who already sap the strength of the State for these lesser sacrifices ... in order to prevent our being swamped with incompetence. It is better for all the world*, if instead of waiting to execute degenerate offspring for crime, or to let them starve for their imbecility, *society* can prevent those who are *manifestly unfit from continuing their kind*. The principle that sustains compulsory vaccination is broad enough to cover cutting the Fallopian tubes. *Three generations of*

imbeciles are enough. [Emphasis and bracketed words are mine.]

Thus does Holmes's opinion reek of a defense of eugenics.[1] It has been estimated that as many as 70,000 Americans, men and women alike, were sterilized until 1944, most of them because of the widespread belief that eugenics was a solution to reduce reproduction of certain "undesirables."[2]

Buck v. *Bell* has never been overruled by the Supreme Court of the United States.

As we shall see, the underlying doctrines that made eugenics fashionable and compulsory sterilization laws possible—altruism, collectivism, and statism—are what today prevent Americans from possessing independent control over their deaths.

1.

INTRODUCTION

In 1997 the Supreme Court of the United States unanimously ruled in *Washington* v. *Glucksberg*[3] that there was no federal constitutional right that would allow a competent terminal adult patient to commit suicide.[4] (I choose not to describe the most personal act a human being can perform, suicide, as "ending one's life," "checking out," "self- termination," or any other euphemism. The most appropriate word, and the act itself, is "suicide.")

In so ruling, the Supreme Court "strictly scrutinized" the Washington State Physician Assisted Death statute. The Court applied traditional Fourteenth Amendment "due process" and "fundamental rights" analysis, which included use of various "tests."

However, in the context of right-to-die legislation such as the State of Washington's, those tests were *ad hoc*, subjective, and they "balanced" individual rights and the right to die against the pernicious doctrines of altruism, collectivism, and statism, all in service of the "common good."

I wrote this book to expose how and why the Supreme Court in *Glucksberg* reached its unanimous, morally wrong, constitutionally indefensible, and potentially dangerous decision, and to expose the foundation of altruism, collectivism, and statism that were the decision's underlying doctrines.

As we shall see, the Supreme Court's methodology is not consistent, principled, and defensible rights-based constitutional analysis and adjudication. It is, instead, judicial policymaking that eschews proper Originalist[5] constitutional judicial review.

There is, however, a different constitutional analysis available, one which comports with the "self-evident" truths that "all men ... are endowed ... with certain unalienable Rights, that among these are Life, Liberty and the pursuit of Happiness. That to secure these rights, Governments are instituted among men, deriving their just *powers from the consent of the governed... .* "[6] [Emphasis mine.]

That different analysis is the only legitimate way to recognize and secure an individual's moral and constitutional right to die.

2.

DEFINITIONS

Lest there be any misunderstanding about how I define the words and concepts "altruism, collectivism, and statism" in this book, they are set forth below, with their sources.

> Altruism. "The basic principle of altruism is that man has no right to exist for his own sake, that service to others is the only justification of his existence, and that self-sacrifice is his highest moral duty, virtue and value. * * * The issue is whether the need of others is the first mortgage on your life and the moral purpose of your existence. The issue is whether man is to be regarded as a sacrificial animal." (Ayn Rand, "Faith and Force: The Destroyers of the Modern World," Philosophy: Who Needs It (1982), 72.).

> "Altruism declares that any action taken for the benefit of others is good, and any action taken for one's benefit is evil. Thus, the *beneficiary* of an action is the only criterion of moral value—and so long as that beneficiary is anybody other than oneself, anything goes." (Ayn Rand, "Introduction," *The Virtue of Selfishness,* x.) [Emphasis in original.]

> "Now there is one word—a single word—which can blast the morality of altruism out of existence and which it

cannot withstand—the word: '*Why?*' Why must man live for the sake of others? *Why* must he be a sacrificial animal? *Why* is that the good? There is no earthly reason for it—and ... in the whole history of philosophy no *earthly* reason has ever been given." (Ayn Rand, "Faith and Force: The Destroyers of the Modern World," Philosophy: Who Needs It (1982), 74). [Emphasis in original.]

"Why is it moral to serve the happiness of others, but not your own?" (Ayn Rand, "Galt's Speech," *For the New Intellectual*, 178.)

Collectivism "means the subjugation of the individual to a group—whether to a race, class or State does not matter. Collectivism holds that man must be chained to collective action and collective thought for the sake of what is called 'the common good'." ["The common good" is defined below.] (Ayn Rand, "The Only Path to Tomorrow," *Reader's Digest*, January 1944, 8.)

"Collectivism holds that in human affairs, the collective—society, the community, the nation, the proletariat, the race, etc.—is *the unit of reality and the standard of value*. On this view, the individual has reality only as a part of the group, and value only insofar as he serves it." (Leonard Peikoff, *The Ominous Parallels* (1982), 7. [Emphasis in original.]

"Collectivism holds that the individual has no rights, that his life and work belong to the group ... and the group may sacrifice him at its own whim to its own interests. The only way to implement a doctrine of that kind is by means of brute force—and *statism* has always been the political corollary of collectivism." (Ayn Rand, "Racism," *The Virtue of Selfishness*, 175).

Statism. "holds that man's life and work belong to the State—to society, to the group, the gang, the race, the nation—and that the State may dispose of him in any way it pleases for the sake of whatever it deems to be its own tribal, collective good." (Ayn Rand, "Introducing Objectivism," *The Objectivist Newsletter*, August 1962, 35.)

"Government control of a country's economy—any kind or degree of such control, by any group, for any purpose whatsoever—rests on the basic principle of *statism*, the principle that man's life belongs to the State." (Ayn Rand, "Conservatism: An Obituary," *Capitalism, the Unknown Ideal* (1966, 193).

"[T]he term "statism" designates concentration of power in the State at the expense of individual liberty." (Leonard Peikoff, *The Ominous Parallels* (1962), 6.)

"The ideological root of statism (or collectivism) is the *tribal premise* of primordial savages who, unable to conceive of individual rights, believed that the tribe is a supreme, omnipotent ruler, that it owns the lives of its members and may sacrifice them whenever it pleases to whatever it believes to be its own 'good'." (Ayn Rand, "The Roots of War," *Capitalism, the Unknown Ideal* (1966), 192.

Common good. "The tribal notion of 'the common good' has served as the moral justification of most social systems—and of all tyrannies—in history."

"When 'the common good' of a society is regarded as something apart from and superior to the individual good of its members, it means that the good of *some* men takes precedence over the good of others, with those others consigned to the status of sacrificial animals. It is tacitly assumed, in such cases, that 'the common good' means 'the good of the *majority*' as against the minority or the individual." (Ayn Rand, "What is Capitalism," *Capitalism, the Unknown Ideal* (1966), 20.) [Emphasis in original.]

"Only on the basis of individual rights can any good—private or public—be defined and achieved. Only when each man is free to exist for his own sake—neither sacrificing others to himself nor being sacrificed to others—only then is every man free to work for the greatest good he can achieve for himself by his own choice and by his own effort. And the total of such individual efforts is the only kind of general, social good possible." (Ayn Rand, Textbook of Americanism, pamphlet, 11.)

3.

HISTORICAL CONTEXT

Thomas Jefferson's "Laws of Nature and of Nature's God"[7] that endowed our unalienable rights, are expressed in the first nine amendments to the Bill of Rights of the Constitution of the United States of America.[8]

The right to life, liberty, and the pursuit of happiness of which Jefferson wrote in the Declaration of Independence and which was then textually enumerated in the Bill of Rights, today survives mostly in watered-down versions. The First Amendment protection of speech is riddled with exceptions for defamation, pornography, fighting words, commercial speech, and more. The Second Amendment right to bear arms has been narrowed into protecting only gun ownership in one's residence for self-defense. The Fourth Amendment requirement of probable cause yielded to the exception for "plain view" and "expectation of privacy." The Fifth Amendment's promise that no private property may be "taken for public use" has been amended by Supreme Court decisions so that "public use" now means "public purpose." Other amendments, such as the Sixth and Eighth, have suffered the same fate.

How did this happen?

4.

MAGNA CARTA; FOURTEENTH AMENDMENT; PROCEDURAL DUE PROCESS

At the Constitutional Convention of 1787, delegates expressed great wariness about the creation of a powerful federal government.

Despite that concern, when two of the delegates, Elbridge Gerry and George Mason, tried to introduce the subject of a "bill of rights" they were unsuccessful, even though some state constitutions already contained bills of rights in one form or another.

The subject of a bill of rights raged among the citizenry in the state ratification debates and in the press. Much of the opposition to the proposed Constitution was based on its lack of a bill of rights. Alexander Hamilton's *The Federalist 84* made a convincing case against a bill of rights:

> It has been several times truly remarked that bills of rights are, in their origin, stipulations between kings and their subjects, abridgements of prerogative in favor of privilege, reservations of rights not surrendered to the prince. Such was Magna Carta obtained by the barons, sword in hand, from King John. Such were the subsequent confirmations of that charter by succeeding princes. Such

was the *Petition of Right* assented to by Charles I, in the beginning of his reign. Such, also, was the Declaration of Right presented by the Lords and Commons to the Prince of Orange in 1688, and afterwards thrown into the form of an act of parliament called the Bill of Rights. It is evident, therefore, that, according to their primitive signification, they have no application to constitutions professedly founded upon the power of the people, and executed by their immediate representatives and servants. [Emphasis in original.]

Here, in strictness, the people surrender nothing; and as they retain everything, they have no need of particular reservations. "WE, THE PEOPLE of the United States, to secure the blessings of liberty to ourselves and our posterity, do *ordain* and *establish* this Constitution for the United States of America." Here is a better recognition of popular rights, than volumes of those aphorisms which make the principal figure in several of our State bills of rights, and which would sound much better in a treatise of ethics than in a constitution of government. [My emphasis; capitalized words in original.]

In other words, Hamilton argued that the Constitution only *delegated power*, so there was no reason expressly to *reserve rights*. If they were expressly reserved, the argument could be made that any rights not expressly reserved were thus not protected. Do not make a list, Hamilton cautioned, because rights not enumerated would arguably not exist.

Hamilton's argument prevailed, and the Constitution was ratified without a bill of rights.

Then, in the First Congress, James Madison brilliantly solved Hamilton's "do not enumerate rights" problem by authoring what became the Ninth Amendment.

Madison also introduced an amendment designed to protect the rights of conscience, press, and criminal jury trial against violation by the *states*. Madison's was an explicit attempt to reach *state* action via prohibitions in the *federal* Bill of Rights, but his proposal was rejected, with the consequence that *the enacted Bill of Rights contains no explicit or implicit prohibitions against the states*. Indeed, the First Amendment begins with the unequivocal statement that *"Congress* shall make no law." [My emphasis.]

Considering the explicit rejection of Madison's "state" amendment, the first word of Article I of the Bill of Rights, and the universal understanding in 1791 about the *federal* nature of amendments First through Ninth, there is no doubt that the Bill of Rights was intended, and written, to apply only to the federal government.

Indeed, in the 1833 case of *Barron* v. *Baltimore*,[9] some forty-two years after the 1791 promulgation of the Bill of Rights, the Supreme Court expressly ruled that the first ten amendments applied only to the federal government. There were still judges and others alive in 1791 when the First Congress adopted the Bill of Rights, and they knew very well what its purpose and scope was intended to be.

Among the various amendments, the Fifth provided that "[n]o person shall ... be deprived of life, liberty, or property without *due process of law*... ." [My emphasis.]

The source of the Fifth Amendment's Due Process Clause was Magna Carta's Stipulation 39 (of 63). There, English King John agreed that "[n]o freemen shall be taken or imprisoned or disseised [dispossessed] or exiled or in any way destroyed, nor will we go upon him nor send upon him, except by the lawful judgment of his peers or *by the law of the land*." [My emphasis.]

According to *Black's Law Dictionary*, "[b]y the law of the land is most clearly intended the general law which *hears before it condemns*, which *proceeds upon inquiry*, and renders *judgment only after trial.* * * * The meaning is that every citizen shall hold his life, liberty, property, and immunities under the protection of general rules which govern society." [My emphasis.]

This definition speaks only of *procedure*, not substance: *how* a law is to be enforced, not whether the law is *proper*, *legal*, or *constitutional*. *Due process / law of the land* speaks of *process*, not *substance*.

It was from the principle of "by the law of the land" that the early concept of due *process* of law evolved: "No man of what State or condition he be, shall be put out of his lands or tenements nor taken, nor disinherited, nor put to death, without he be brought to answer by due *process* of law," said an A.D. 1355 English restatement of the A.D. 1215 Magna Carta. [My emphasis.]

Just as Magna Carta, the A.D. 1215 English statute, and early American state constitutions with similar provisions make abundantly clear, "due process of law" related exclusively to fair *procedure*.

I emphasize the *procedural* nature of due process because *procedure* is wholly different from *substance*. Whether an accused has the right to an indictment first, rather than summary trial (procedure), is different from whether as a matter of public policy a legislature possesses the legal and constitutional power to make prostitution a crime (substance). This important distinction between procedure and substance would become crucial and contribute substantially to the ruination of American constitutional law. The resolution of the ensuing argument changed the United States radically. We have never recovered.

If there is any doubt about the *procedural* nature of due process, we need only examine the Fifth Amendment's positioning in the overall architecture of the Bill of Rights.

The Fourth Amendment deals exclusively with the criminal *procedure* of searches and seizures.

The Fifth Amendment—where the federal Due Process Clause is found—deals exclusively with four other *procedural* protections, three of which are indictment, double jeopardy, and self-incrimination.

The Sixth Amendment deals, *procedurally*, with speedy and public trials, impartial jury, notice of the nature and cause of charges, confrontation by witnesses, compulsory process, and assistance of counsel.

This architecture, along with history beginning with Magna Carta in A.D. 1215 and its restatement in A.D. 1355, leaves no doubt that our Constitution's Fifth Amendment's due process protection was intended by the Founders to be solely of a *procedural* nature and to operate only against the *federal* government.

There is no better explication of procedural due process than in the case of *Jones* v. *Flowers*, where Associate Justice Clarence Thomas dissented.[10] First the facts of the *Jones* case:

> When ... [Jones] failed to pay his property taxes for several consecutive years, [the] Commissioner of State Lands in Arkansas, using the record address that Jones provided to the State, *sent Jones a letter by certified mail*, noting his tax delinquency and explaining that his property would be subject to public sale if the delinquent taxes and penalties were not paid. After [Jones] *failed to respond*, the State also *published notice* of the delinquency and public sale in an Arkansas newspaper. Soon after ... Linda K. Flowers submitted a purchase offer to the State, it sent [Jones] a *second letter by certified mail* explaining that the sale would proceed if the delinquent taxes and penalties were not paid.
>
> [Jones] argues that the State violated his rights under the Due Process Clause of the Fourteenth Amendment because, in [Jones's] view, the State failed to take sufficient steps to contact him before selling his property to Flowers. [Jones] contends that once the State became aware that he had not claimed the certified mail, it was

constitutionally obligated [by due process] to employ additional methods to locate him. [My emphasis.]

The question for the Supreme Court was whether Fourteenth Amendment *procedural due process* of law requires that "when mailed notice of a tax sale is returned unclaimed, the State must take additional reasonable steps to attempt to provide notice to the property owner before selling his property, if it is practicable to do so." The 5–3 Supreme Court majority's answer was "yes."

Unfortunately for the Court's reputation, especially because the majority opinion was written by Chief Justice John Roberts, one hunts in vain for a reason *why* the Due Process Clause of the Fourteenth Amendment required Arkansas to do more than it did.

Roberts and his four predictably liberal colleagues believed that because the stakes were high—Jones's loss of his home—the state *should* have done more simply because it *could* have done more. This was a *legislative policy* ruling by the Court, not a legal decision based on the clear meaning and history of procedural due process. There was, and is, a profoundly important distinction between *legislative policy* and *judicial originalism*, as conceived and implemented by the Founders.

Justice Thomas dissented in *Flowers* and shredded Roberts's majority opinion.

Thomas began by referring to various Court precedents:

> Balancing a state's interest in efficiently managing its administrative system and an individual's interest in adequate notice, this Court has held that a State must provide notice reasonably calculated, under all the circumstances, to apprise interested parties of the pendency of the action."

Okay, that makes sense. Fair procedure is important. *Process* is important.

Justice Thomas continued:

> The methods of *notice* employed by Arkansas were reasonably calculated to *inform* [Jones] of *proceedings* [above emphasis, Thomas] affecting his property interest and thus satisfy the requirements of the Due Process Clause. The State mailed a *notice* by *certified* letter to the address provided by petitioner. The certified letter was returned to the State marked 'unclaimed' after *three* attempts to deliver it. The State then *published a notice* of public sale containing redemption information in the Arkansas Democrat Gazette newspaper. After Flowers submitted a purchase offer, the State sent yet *another certified letter* to petitioner at his record address. That letter, too, was returned to the State marked 'unclaimed' after *three* delivery attempts." [Other emphasis mine.]

Notice that Justice Thomas's focus ("notice," "inform," "proceedings") was on *procedure*, not substance.

But what about someone admitting that a *procedure* is constitutional, but complaining that the *substance* of the law is not? That, for example, a thousand-dollar fine for a parking ticket is unconstitutional *substantively* under the Eighth Amendment's prohibition of "excessive fines"? Or that protest parades of more than fifty marchers are illegal, despite the First Amendment's guarantees of free speech and assembly? Or that a state ban on purchase and use of contraceptives is unconstitutional under some constitutional provision or other? How would those alleged unconstitutional laws, and countless other state laws, be tested for their constitutional legitimacy?

These questions bring me to one of the Supreme Court's worst inventions: The "substantive" due process doctrine, a crucial tool of judicial denial that Americans own our lives, and thus possess the unalienable moral and constitutional right to commit suicide.

5.

"SUBSTANTIVE" DUE PROCESS

The first American state legislatures had considerable power, especially over property rights. For example, anti-creditor confiscation laws and floods of paper-money, which reduced the purchasing power of creditors and fostered inflation.

The new federal judiciary of mostly federalists wanted to stop the predatory state legislation. How to do it? Rather than relying on the Constitution, the judges invoked extra-constitutional principles, such as those found in the "natural law" writings of English philosopher John Locke and others.

For example, in 1795, four years after the Bill of Rights was enacted, Justice William Paterson of the new Supreme Court of the United States wrote in the case of *Vanhorne's Lessee* v. *Dorrance*:[11]

> The right of acquiring and possessing property, and having it protected, is one of the *natural, inherent,* and *unalienable* rights of man. Men have a sense of property: Property is necessary to their subsistence, and correspondent to their natural wants and desires; its security was one of the objects that induced them to unite in society. No man would become a member of a community in which he could not enjoy the fruits of his honest labour and industry. The preservation of property

then is a primary object of the social compact, and, by the late Constitution of *Pennsylvania*, was made a *fundamental* law.

Every person ought to contribute his proportion for public purposes and public exigencies; but no one can be called upon to surrender or *sacrifice* his whole property, real and personal, *for the good of the community*, without receiving a recompence in value. This would be laying a burden upon an individual, which ought to be sustained by the *society* at large.

The English history does not furnish an instance of the kind; the Parliament, with all their boasted omnipotence, never committed such an outrage on private property; and if they had, it would have served only to display the dangerous nature of unlimited authority; it would have been an exercise of power and not of right. Such an act would be a monster in legislation, and shock all mankind. The legislature, therefore, had no authority to make *an act divesting one citizen of his freehold, and vesting it in another*, without a just compensation. *It is inconsistent with the principles of reason, justice, and moral rectitude*; it is incompatible with the comfort, peace, and happiness of mankind; it is contrary to the principles of social alliance in every free government; and lastly, it is contrary both to the letter and spirit of the Constitution. [Spelling as in the original. The word "Pennsylvania" was emphasized in the original. All other emphasis is mine.]

As rousing as Justice Paterson's words were, many believed that while the Court's reliance on "the letter ... of the Constitution" would suffice as the basis of a pro-property decision *if* an appropriate Constitutional provision could be found, the Supreme Court of the United States should better support its ruling than to base it on virtually meaningless abstract "principles of reason, justice, and moral rectitude," "the comfort, peace, and happiness of mankind," and "the principles of social alliance in every free government." Let alone on the "spirit of the Constitution." These empty slogans—as rousing, patriotic, and heartfelt as they were, and whatever they meant— were *non-constitutional*. Some textual *Constitutional* basis was thought necessary.

As the right to vote became more widespread and the power of legislatures grew, property and contract rights became more threatened. Those rights were being sacrificed to the collective's need for such things as soft money, debtor relief laws, and other forcible altruist, collectivist, statist transfers of private property.

In response, a firmer basis was sought upon which to ground judicial protection of property and contract rights. Ideally, by some *specific textual Constitutional provisions*, state and federal. The goal was to move the protection of private rights—liberty, property, contract—away from the popularly elected legislatures and put them in the courts, where it was hoped lawyers and judges would protect such rights.

But how? How to defend on purely *constitutional* grounds by relying on the constitutions themselves? Recall that on the federal level, the sole provision of the Bill of Rights that mentioned the word "property" was the *procedural* Due Process Clause of the Fifth Amendment.

This reality sat atop a slippery slope. Because some textual constitutional justification was sought, and because the Due Process Clause of the Fifth Amendment—"No person shall ... be deprived of life, liberty, or property without due process of law"—was the only place in the Bill of Rights where property was mentioned, that procedural amendment was chosen to carry the burden of determining whether government action was "substantively" constitutional.

By what objective constitutional standard no one knew, because from Magna Carta until the 1800s due process clauses had always applied only to *form, process, procedure*. Manifestly, *never* to substance.

But how would this mutation of procedural due process become accepted constitutional doctrine, especially since everyone knew "due process" was synonymous only with procedure?

How was *procedural* due process to be transmogrified into a *substantive* tool by which the *content* of legislation could be judged? A tool that would enable courts to decide the undefined "rightness" or "wrongness" of legislation based solely on the policy values of judges?

How were the *policy* choices—social, economic, fiscal, cultural, political, sexual—of *politically accountable legislatures* to be evaluated for their constitutionality by *politically unaccountable judges*?

For example, by what criteria was a court to decide, not whether a defendant could be tried for gambling in a court where the judge was prosecutor and jury (which would be a *procedural* deprivation of the defendant's *procedural* rights), but instead whether the legislature possessed the legal or constitutional power to make gambling illegal at all (a substantive question).

Understanding this distinction between procedural and substantive due process is essential to understanding what the Supreme Court has done to individual rights, limited government, capitalism, and, fundamentally, the right to die.

So, let's slide a bit further down the slippery slope.

In the mid-1800s, New York enacted a statewide liquor prohibition law (which included destruction of existing stocks) and applied it *retroactively* to liquor already in existence when the law was passed. Property rights in existing legal inventories of liquor were destroyed.

In the New York Court of Appeals, the majority opinion in the case of *Wynehamer* v. *The People of the State of New York*[12] was written by Judge George Comstock. He rightly and expressly repudiated all the arguments made against the prohibition law based on "fundamental liberty," "common sense," "natural law" and "natural rights," none of which found textual support in either the constitution or statutes of the State of New York.

To the contrary, Comstock wrote that there was nothing *outside* the state constitution to render the prohibition law unconstitutional that couldn't also be found *inside* the state constitution: "[T]here is no process of reasoning by which it can be demonstrated that [the prohibition law] is void upon principles and theories outside the [New York] constitution, which will not also and by an easier deduction, bring it in direct conflict with the [New York] constitution itself."

In other words, people whose property (or liberty, or contracts) had been taken from them should not have to seek protection in "fundamental liberty," common sense," "natural law," or "natural rights." There was *textual* protection, Judge Comstock found, in the constitution of the State of New York itself.

By now, the reader need not guess what part of the New York constitution Judge Comstock was alluding to in his "outside-inside" analysis.

New York's constitution contained a due process clause, which, like others elsewhere, was exclusively *procedural*. No matter. Comstock would protect against the retroactive confiscation of Mr. Wynehamer's legal liquor by invoking "due process," not procedurally, but *substantively*.

But due process of law had never been employed by the New York courts as the means to determine the *substance* of a statute, to somehow decide whether a law was "right," "wrong," "moral," "commonsensical," "stupid," "brilliant," or otherwise acceptable or unacceptable, by some standard or other. Let alone whether it was constitutional or unconstitutional.

No matter.

The New York Court of Appeals ruled that the law violated due process of law, which could only mean that New York's constitutional provision had been applied to *substance*.

The next year, invoking the federal Fifth Amendment, the amoeba-like division of procedural due process into one part itself and another part substantive due process became a reality in the morally corrupt, legally and constitutionally indefensible *federal* case of *Dred Scott v. Sandford*.[13]

Chief Justice Roger B. Taney ruled that Section 8 of the Missouri Compromise, *excluding* slavery from the new American territories, was void under the Fifth Amendment. Not because the *procedure* for enacting or enforcing the law did not afford "due process," but because the Supreme Court of the United States regarded as *unjust* the inability of slave owners to take their "property" (i.e., slaves) from one place to another. Said the Chief Justice for the Court majority,

> [A]n act of Congress which deprives a citizen of *his liberty or property* [!], merely because he came himself or brought his property into a particular territory of the United States and who had committed no offense against the laws could hardly be dignified with the name of *due process of law*. [My emphasis.]

Thus, in its 7–2 *Dred Scott* decision, the Supreme Court of the United States declared that slavery was constitutional in the territories because Section 8 of the Missouri Compromise was "unfair," "unjust," "unreasonable," "inequitable." Choose any synonym. It was just not "right," by whatever subjective standard Chief Justice Taney and his six colleagues invoked (if they had any standard at all).

The *Dred Scott* decision "legitimized," at least *federally*, the Fifth Amendment's Due Process Clause as possessing substantive power to invalidate laws enacted by *Congress*. The writing was on the wall: the Due Process and Law of the Land Clauses that since Magna Carta in A.D. 1215 had been utilized to consecrate specific modes of *procedure* had been judicially transformed into a subjective monitor of any legislation capable of having a detrimental effect on individual rights.

The result of *Dred Scott* was that seven members of the Supreme Court of the United States, *based on their own policy values*, opened vast new territorial lands to the immorality and unconstitutionality of slavery, despite Congress having expressly prohibited it. The Supreme Court accepted that a slave could be someone else's "property," that the "master's" ownership was an ingredient of the latter's "liberty," and to deprive the "master" of his "property" violated the previously non-existent "substantive" portion of the United States Constitution's Fifth Amendment Due Process Clause.

Accordingly, the *Dred Scott* decision opened the courthouse doors to a doctrine which, when fully developed, was, and continues to be, destructive of individual rights and a pernicious prohibition of the right to die.

But *Dred Scott* was a *federal* case. What about the states?

Time for some historical context.

In the time of the *Wynehamer* state and *Dred Scott* federal cases, there was an important political development afoot in the United States. Those cases and other judicial decisions like them, were jurisprudential fodder for the spread of Jacksonian democracy. This newly articulated doctrine of "popular sovereignty" trumpeted the supremacy of legislatures. *Vox Populi*, "The Voice of the People."

With good reason, many Americans considered this trend extremely dangerous. Governments were dabbling financially in railroads, canals, manufacturing, banks, steamships, and many other commercial activities. Because creditors and other owners of property were justifiably concerned about the nearly unlimited power of state legislatures, they turned for help to the courts.

But there was a serious obstacle beyond that of the substantive due process problem. The only Due Process Clause was in the *federal Bill of Rights' Fifth Amendment*, which restrained only the *federal* government, not the *states*. Unlike New York, not every state constitution had a Due Process Clause.

Then, in 1868, American constitutional law, the protection of individual rights, and the Founders' attempted institutionalization of limited government by means of strictly delegated powers, their separation and legitimate judicial review, changed forever.

The Fourteenth Amendment was ratified on July 9, 1868:

> [N]or shall any *State* deprive any person of life, liberty, or property, without *due process of law*." [My emphasis.]

Now courts could apply substantive due process analysis not only to laws enacted by Congress, as in *Dred Scott*, but also to *state* legislation via the Fourteenth Amendment. In time they did.

A century later, I reviewed a book by Harvard Law School Professor Raoul Berger, entitled *Government by Judiciary: The Transformation of the Fourteenth Amendment*.[14] Here is my introduction to the substantive due process phenomenon on the state level which, as we'll see, has so negatively affected the "right-to-die" battle:

> Raoul Berger has written one of the most important books in the literature of American constitutional law, and one of the most disturbing. The book's first sentence expresses his thesis, drawn from his exhaustive examination of the Fourteenth Amendment's background and legislative history: The Fourteenth Amendment is the case study par excellence of what [the first] Justice Harlan described as the Supreme Court's "exercise of the amending power," its *continuing revision of the Constitution under the guise of interpretation*. [My emphasis.]

In *Government by Judiciary*, Professor Berger proved conclusively that the Fourteenth Amendment's Due Process Clause was intended to deal with the same *procedural* deprivation of rights as was the federal Fifth Amendment's Due Process Clause, whose development and application began with Magna Carta centuries earlier.

In the *Brooklyn Law Review*, I wrote that "Berger piles proof upon proof to demonstrate that neither in 1787 [the Constitution] nor in 1868 [the Fourteenth Amendment] did due process 'comprehend judicial power to override legislation on substantive or *policy* grounds.'"

Following ratification of the Fourteenth Amendment, every state law, especially those allegedly affecting individual rights were fair game for anyone wanting to attack the law based on the Fourteenth Amendment's now-*substantive* Due Process Clause.

However, despite *Dred Scott*, *Wynehamer*, and some similar state cases, the Supreme Court majority refused for many years to apply the Due Process Clause of the Fourteenth Amendment to anything except alleged *procedural* deprivations of rights. Those Courts knew better.

But there were murmurs. The pot was bubbling. Litigants were aware of how "substantive due process" arguments might help them. Lawyers discussed them. Articles appeared in professional literature. A movement began.

In 1878, ten years after the enactment of the Fourteenth Amendment, a case entitled *Davidson* v. *New Orleans* [15] reached the Supreme Court of the United States. Justice Samuel Miller wrote for the majority:

> While the Fourteenth Amendment has been part of the Constitution, as a restraint upon the power of the State, in only a very few years the docket of this court is crowded with cases in which we are asked to hold that State courts and State legislatures have deprived their own citizens of life, liberty, or property without due process of law.
>
> *There is here abundant evidence that there exists some strange misconception of the scope of this provision as*

> *found in the Fourteenth Amendment.* In fact, it would seem, from the character of many of the cases before us, and the arguments made in them, that the clause under consideration, due process, is looked upon as a means of bringing to the test of the decision of this court *the abstract opinions of every unsuccessful litigant in a State court the justice of the decision against him, and of the merits of the legislation on which such a decision may be founded.* [My emphasis.]

Despite Justice Miller's analysis, there continued to be pro-substantive due process dissents in various cases. Finally, in the late 1800s, the earlier substantive due process dissents finally became majority law. In *Mugler* v. *Kansas*,[16] the Supreme Court majority ruled that due process had substantive clout and could subjectively test the "fairness," "reasonableness," "justness" of state legislation, based, of course, on the personal policy values of judges because there was no objective standard.

The first Justice John Harlan wrote:

> It does not at all follow that every statute enacted ostensibly for the promotion of these ends, that is police power and health, safety, welfare, and morals, is to be accepted as a legitimate exercise of the powers of the State.

True.

> There are, of necessity, limits beyond which legislation cannot rightfully go.

True, again.

> While every possible presumption is to be indulged in favor of the validity of the statute, the courts must obey the Constitution rather than the law-making department of the government [the legislature], and must, upon their own responsibility, determine whether, in any particular case, these limits have been passed.

Again, true.

But by what criteria are the limits to be ascertained and then applied?

Here is one answer. In the 1890 case of *Chicago, Milwaukee & St. Paul Railway Company* v. *Minnesota*,[17] the Supreme Court ruled that the validity of railroad rates fixed by state administrative commissions were not final. Their "reasonableness" was a matter for judicial review. Why? The Court ruled that if rates were "unreasonable," the railroad was deprived of the lawful use of its property and thus of the property itself, without—guess what? —*substantive due process of law. Why*, the Court did not explain.

The constitutional standard by which to assess government interference with rights had become "reasonableness" in the eyes of the judicial beholders. Individual rights were now to be protected, or not, throughout the United States of America by this policy-driven, subjective, standardless judicial invention.

Two years later, in 1892, at the American Bar Association's annual meeting, the general counsel of a major railroad delivered a paper entitled "Limitations on the legislative power in respect to personal rights and private property." What did he support? Why, of course, he was a staunch fighter for the "right" of railroads to make "reasonable" profits—a determination, he said, for *judicial* rather than *legislative* determination. Well, with friends like him, American business did not need enemies, though it had plenty.

Note what had happened. Seeking protection from state legislative excesses, conservative lawyers attempted to shift their battles into the courts, where the traditional *procedural* due process clauses would acquire *substantive* meaning and test the "reasonableness" of those alleged excesses. Altruist-collectivist-statist legislation would be judged by subjective standards such as "reasonableness," most of the time reflecting the personal values of the hopefully conservative judges. But the corporate lawyers miscalculated, failing to realize that substantive due process was a two-way street. Though attributed to Lenin, it was Karl Marx who said, "The last capitalist we hang shall be the one who sold us the rope." The lawyers had sold the country "substantive due process, and they would be hanged by it."

The sad truth is that proponents of substantive due process were trading short-term gains for long-term jurisprudential instability and destruction of the very values of individual rights they naively thought they were protecting. It was not only that they did not know what they were doing, which was bad enough. Worse, the values of most of them were the same altruist-collectivist-statist values they thought they were fighting.

In the 1898 case of *Smyth* v. *Ames*,[18] the Court ruled public utilities had the "right" to "reasonable profits," a "fair return." If anyone asked embarrassing questions—such as "Reasonable to whom?" "Why?" "For how long?" "How much?" "By what standard?"—no meaningful answer was forthcoming.

Few of the conservative businessmen, lawyers, and judges who heralded what they called the "new constitutional mandate" for laissez-faire apparently realized, or cared about, the destructive idea they were advancing. Profit deemed "reasonable" by one court in 1898 might well be deemed "unreasonable" by another court on another day, or in another decade. Nor did they realize the implications of "reasonable profits" defined not by capitalism's free market, but by a legislature or a court. Or, worse, by an administrative agency.

Liberty and economic rights were to be protected not because they were absolute, not because they were inalienable, and not because government had no right to violate them. Not because they were individual rights inherited from Jefferson, Madison, Hamilton, and the other Founders. Instead, rights were going to be protected, or not, depending on whether interference with them would be deemed "unreasonable" by a court. They would be protected by a legal fiction, a judicial invention called "substantive due process of law," by a standard of "reasonableness," "justness," or "unjustness." There was no *objective* standard of what was, and what was not, reasonable, much less what "rights" were. Fundamental rights were to be sacrificed on the altar of altruism, collectivism, and statism.

That said, let's look at a case that exemplifies the toxic combination of substantive due process and altruism, collectivism, and statism. With an apology to Charles Dickens, here is the Supreme Court case of *Muller* v. *Oregon*.[19]

It is December 1902 in London, Oregon. Cold and snowing. Sixteen-year-old Emma Gotcher needs money for Christmas because the family anticipates that all they will get from her father's employer is a lump of coal, and they want to buy little Tiny Tim, a sled. Emma goes looking for work and comes upon a "help wanted" sign outside the Grand Laundry. She tells the manager that she needs work because poor crippled Tiny Tim will be devastated if he does not get a sled for Christmas.

"Well," says the manager, "I'll tell you what; we've got work for a starcher.[20] But it's fifteen-hour-a-day work, it's hard, and you're going to have to stand most of the time." "That's acceptable," says Emma, "I don't care. I have to get the family get that sled for Tiny Tim." Muller says, "Well, that's great."

Note that each party was thrilled. The family could give Tiny Tim a sled for Christmas. Boss Muller would have a starcher. A win-win situation. A voluntarily formed contract. Capitalism, the free market, and liberty of contract at work.

But not for long.

A few months later, the Oregon Legislature, in its wisdom and looking out for the generic "little woman," enacted a law whose first section said: "No female shall be employed in any mechanical establishment or factory or laundry in this State more than 10 hours in any one day." If a female was so employed, the employer would be guilty of a misdemeanor.

Uh-oh.[21]

In September 1905, the laundry's owner was charged with violating the statute. He was convicted and fined.

Eventually, the case of *Muller* v. *Oregon* reached the Supreme Court of the United States. There, the question for the justices was whether a healthy American woman in the early twentieth century could freely choose to work more than ten hours a day, whatever her reasons, or whether "government" (in this case, the State of Oregon) knew better what was good for Emma Gotcher and other girls and women in a similar position. Whether the government could sacrifice her needs and rights to the policy values of her friends and neighbors, also known as "society, Emma lost her salary, Mr. Muller paid a fine. Tiny Tim did not get his sled.

But by enacting the statute, the altruists, collectivists, and statists did a good deed by "helping" Emma Gotcher and all women in Oregon similarly situated.

The Supreme Court of the United States upheld the Oregon statute, to the loud cheers of the progressives of that day who applauded the justices' enlightened concern for working women who apparently either did not know, or could not protect, their own interests, as construed by the Oregon voters, legislature, governor, and state courts (i.e., "society.")

But if the decision's partisans, especially women, had paid attention to the Court's reasons for its decision in *Muller* v. *Oregon*, they probably would not have cheered so loudly, if at all. Indeed, if they really understood the decision, they should have been appalled. Even scared.

Muller v. *Oregon* was a *unanimous* decision, one that today's feminists, progressives, socialists, and such others should take no comfort from. To quote the Court:

> That woman's physical structure and the performance of maternal functions places her at a disadvantage in the struggle for subsistence is obvious. This is especially

> true when the *burdens of motherhood* are upon her. Even when they are not ... continuance for a long time on her feet at work ... tends to injurious effects upon the body, and, as *healthy mothers are essential to vigorous offspring, the physical well-being of women becomes an object of public interest and care in order to preserve the strength and vigor of the race.* [My emphasis.]

This patronizing view of American working women was not all the Court had to say about the weakness of women and their relationship and sacrificial duty to a paternalistic state.

> Still again, history discloses the fact that *woman has always been dependent upon man.* He established his control at the outset by superior physical strength, and this control in various forms ... has continued to the present. * * * It is still true that in the struggle for subsistence *she is not an equal competitor* with her brother [meaning, any man]. Though limitations upon personal and contractual rights may be removed by legislation, *there is that in her disposition and habits of life which will operate against a full assertion of those rights.* [My emphasis.]

It was bad enough that in upholding the statute the United States Supreme Court, which allegedly was concerned about "subsistence," was limiting the working hours of those trying to subsist. Much worse was the Court's view of working women as weak, timid, and dependent, even cowardly, in being unable or unwilling to assert their "rights." Lest there be any doubt about what the *unanimous* Court was saying:

> [Woman] is so constituted that she will rest upon and look to [man] for protection; that her physical structure and a proper discharge of her maternal functions—having in view not merely her own health, but *the well-being of the race*—justify legislation to protect her from the greed as well as the passion of man. The limitations which this statute places upon her contractual powers, upon her right to agree with her employer as to the time she shall

labor, are not imposed solely for her benefit, *but for the benefit of all.* [My emphasis.]

This is altruism-collectivism-statism run amok.[22]

No doubt some will say that the connection between the Supreme Court's rationale in *Muller* v. *Oregon* and the later Nazi "Master Race" program is, at best, tenuous.

They are mistaken.

To hold women's "physical well-being" and their production of "vigorous offspring" to be matters of "public interest" to "preserve the strength and vigor of the race" is to consider women, as did the Nazis, a mere state resource, important to the government for their procreational capacity, to be nurtured much like livestock, and for the same reason.

The rationale underlying the Supreme Court's decision in *Muller* v. *Oregon* transcends mere altruism, collectivism, and even statism. Such "isms"ultimately deny and negate any possibility of unalienable life, liberty, individual rights, or limited government, or. *And the right to die.*

In *Muller*, the Supreme Court gave voice to a doctrine evil in its intent and murderous in its application: The belief that human beings, in this case women, are mere resources to be used, abused, and ultimately sacrificed for the "common good" by those wielding the power of the State.

The premise upon which *Muller*, its predecessors and progeny rest is that *individuals do not own their own lives*. If they do not, if that premise is a correct reading of the Constitution of the United States of America, it follows that those individuals have no right to terminate their lives when, where, why, and how of their own choosing.

Muller v. *Oregon* was decided by the Supreme Court of the United States in 1908. Less than three decades later, the case's rationale would be evident in Nazi Germany, just as it is in the

Court's *Washington* v. *Glucksberg* condemnation of suicide today.

In those three decades, the final bricks would be put in place by the Supreme Court to complete the jurisprudential edifice that would become known as the "Living Constitution."

It was seen as a great achievement for lawyers and judges to imbue the federal and states' Due Process Clauses with the substantive power to rule on the constitutionality of legislation, but a major question remained.

How could the protections of the federal Bill of Rights—speech, double jeopardy, right of assembly, right to bear arms, and the rest, *which applied against only the federal government*—be made applicable to the states and, coupled with substantive due process, anoint the courts, especially the Supreme Court, as the final arbiters on life, liberty, individual rights, limited government, and capitalism?

It was the *Gitlow* case that put in place the final brick in the edifice of government control of our lives ... and deaths: The "Incorporation Doctrine."

6.

"INCORPORATION" OF THE FOURTEENTH AMENDMENT

An examination of the Incorporation Doctrine begins with an undeniably valid premise: The Bill of Rights was intended by James Madison, who introduced it, the Congress that approved it, and the states that ratified it, to apply only to actions by the *federal* government. Indeed, the First Amendment begins by reciting, "*Congress* shall make no law... ." [My emphasis.]

Never was a political intent, or constitutional language, clearer. So much so that even those who would have it otherwise concede, as they must, that in the early days of the Supreme Court of the United States, the Court ruled squarely that the Bill of Rights was *not* applicable to the states.

How, then, has the Supreme Court been able to hold unconstitutional *under the federal Constitution,* laws of the *states* allegedly violating such rights as free speech, protection against double jeopardy, and many other guarantees found in the *federal* Bill of Rights?

The answer lies in the Due Process Clause of the Fourteenth Amendment's Incorporaton Doctrine: "[N]or shall any *State* deprive any person of life, liberty, or property, without due process of law."

The "Living Constitution" and the Right to Die

Even though the *federal* Bill of Rights contains at least thirty specific "rights" guarantees—one of which is the Fifth Amendment's *own* Due Process Clause—in a series of cases beginning with *Gitlow* v. *New York* [23] in 1925, the Supreme Court ruled that the Fourteenth Amendment's Due Process Clause, which by then had "substantive" content, "incorporated" against the states many of those same federal-like guarantees, thus allowing them to test state legislative action.

It all began with a New York Communist.

At 18, Benjamin Gitlow was a Socialist. At 22, he was the first president of the Retail Clerks, Union of New York, and at 26, Gitlow was elected to the New York State Assembly.

In 1919, socialists of a more revolutionary flavor, like Gitlow and the legendary John Reed, had founded the Communist Labor Party, which later became the Communist Party of the United States. Gitlow ran as the Communist candidate for vice president of the United States in 1924 and 1928. Before his quixotic quest for high political office, Gitlow spent three years in New York's Sing Sing prison on a conviction for violating that state's 1902 criminal anarchy law. That statute wrongly made it a crime to encourage by speech or writing the violent overthrow of the United States government.

Gitlow's indictment contained two counts. The first charged that the defendant had

> *advocated, advised* and *taught* the duty, necessity and propriety of overthrowing and overturning organized government by force, violence and unlawful means, *by* certain *writings* therein set forth entitled "The Left-Wing Manifesto"; the second that he had *printed, published and knowingly circulated and distributed a certain paper* called "The Revolutionary Age," containing the writings set forth in the first count *advocating, advising and teaching* the doctrine that organized government

6. "Incorporation" of the Fourteenth Amendment

should be overthrown by force, violence and unlawful means. [My emphasis.]

Initially at his trial, and later in two New York appellate courts and eventually in the Supreme Court of the United States, Gitlow argued that New York's criminal anarchy statute as written and applied to him violated the Due Process Clause of the Fourteenth Amendment.

But not because there were any *procedural* irregularities in either the law or its application. No, indeed. Gitlow argued that the statute was "substantively" unconstitutional because it punished what Gitlow rightly characterized as "pure speech."

In effect, though not explicitly, Gitlow was invoking the *First Amendment* (which applied only to action by the *federal* government) against a *New York State* law. As we have seen, the *substantive* speech provision of the First Amendment is quite different from the *procedural* Due Process Clause of the Fourteenth Amendment.

Both New York appeals courts held the criminal anarchy statute constitutional.

The Supreme Court of the United States made two rulings.

The more important one set the stage for later "incorporation" of virtually every provision of the Bill of Rights through the Fourteenth Amendment's due process guarantee, thereby endowing that previously purely *procedural* amendment ("due *process*") with the power to test the *substantive* ("rightness," "wrongness," or "reasonableness") content of *all state laws*. The wedding of substantive due process and incorporation proved to be a powerful weapon. Said the Supreme Court:

> For present purposes we may and do *assume* that freedom of speech and of the press—which are protected by the First Amendment from abridgment by *Congress*— are among the *fundamental* personal rights and liberties protected by the due process clause of the Fourteenth

Amendment from impairment by the States. [My emphasis.]

"Assume"!

In other words, lurking somewhere within the Due Process Clause of the Fourteenth Amendment the Court was able to find First Amendment "content," and the former's guarantee that no state shall "deprive any person of life, liberty, or property, without due process of law" really meant that no state shall abridge the kind of freedom of speech found in the First Amendment. And if a state law affecting speech was challenged on the ground that it did abridge free speech, the Supreme Court had the power to assess the *substantive* content of that law (e.g., punishing anarchists' pure speech) to ascertain if it passed constitutional muster, by some standard or other.

That left open the question of what criteria—what test, what standard—the Court could use to decide whether, *substantively*, a state law was constitutional or not.

The *Gitlow* Court continued by observing that there was no absolute right of free speech (or press) even under the First Amendment:

> It is a fundamental principle, long established, that the freedom of speech and of the press which is secured by the Constitution, does not confer an *absolute* right to speak or publish, without responsibility, whatever one may choose, or an unrestricted and unbridled license that gives immunity for every possible use of language and prevents the punishment of those who abuse this freedom. * * * Reasonably *limited* ... this freedom is an inestimable *privilege* in a free government; without such *limitation*, it might become the *scourge of the republic*. [My emphasis.]

So, according to the Supreme Court in 1925, free speech was a mere "privilege," subject to "limitation."

I repeat: But by what *standard? To what or whom can pure speech be subordinated?*

The Supreme Court of the United States was not bashful about its answer:

> That a State in the exercise of its police power may punish those who abuse this freedom by *utterances inimical to the public welfare,* tending to corrupt *public morals,* incite to crime, or disturb the *public peace, is not open to question.* [My emphasis.]

Having concluded that Gitlow's over-the-top Communist ranting was indeed "inimical to the public welfare," the Supreme Court majority upheld his conviction and sentence, adding some hyperbole of its own:

> The State cannot reasonably be required to measure the danger from every such utterance in the nice balance of a jeweler's scale. A single revolutionary spark may kindle a fire that, smoldering for a time, may burst into a sweeping and destructive conflagration.

Even though the United States Supreme Court upheld the New York criminal anarchy statute, and with it Gitlow's conviction, more important for the future of America was that the Court tested the New York law not by the federal Constitution's *Fourteenth* Amendment *procedural* due process provision, but instead, by the *First* Amendment's *substantive* speech protection. The Court did this by *incorporating* First Amendment *substantive* quasi-protection of speech into the Fourteenth Amendment. The essence of the Court's "test" was whether "substantively" the statute was "inimical to the public welfare" and thus constitutionally within New York's power to protect said public.

Gitlow's right to free speech was to be sacrificed (i.e., altruism) to the welfare (i.e., need for security) of others (i.e., the col-

lective) under state law backed by government force via the criminal law (i.e., statism).

Justice Oliver Wendell Holmes authored a dissent for himself and Justice Louis Brandeis. But it was not what one might think. It was not a defense of free speech.

Most interesting about their dissent is that Holmes and Brandeis shared their colleagues' "assumption" that the Fourteenth Amendment's procedural Due *Process* Clause contained First Amendment "content" which, through osmosis-like "incorporation," would be read as part of the Fourteenth Amendment.

Why, then, did they dissent?

Not because they believed New York was powerless to punish subversive speech, for they found no substantive fault with the statute itself. Punishing an anarchist's speech could be "inimical to public welfare."

And not because they believed the Court lacked the judicial power to evaluate the *substantive* content of the statute, for they too *assumed* that the Fourteenth Amendment's Due *Process* Clause could *substantively* test the constitutional appropriateness of the criminal anarchy statute.

Holmes and Brandeis dissented because they disagreed with their colleagues only about whether, *under the facts of that case*, Gitlow's speech was truly "inimical to the public welfare." If it were, he could be sent to Sing Sing prison. If not, he should have been set free. For them, it was a mere fact dispute, a jury question.

For Holmes and Brandeis, those facts were to be evaluated under the test the Court had developed in the earlier World War I free speech case of *Schenck* v. *United States*,[24] where he and others went to prison for protesting conscription. In *Schenck*, Justice Holmes had written for the majority that "[t]he question in every case is whether the words used are used in such circumstances and are of such a nature as to create a *clear and present danger* that they will bring about the *substantive* evils that [the state] has a right to prevent." [My emphasis.]

In *Gitlow*, Holmes and Brandeis thought not. There was, in their opinion, no "clear and present danger." A mere fact dispute, another jury question.

> It is said that this manifesto was more than a theory, that it was an incitement. Every idea is an incitement. It offers itself for belief and if believed it is acted on unless some other belief outweighs it or some failure of energy stifles the movement at its birth. The only difference between the expression of an opinion and an incitement in the narrower sense is the speaker's enthusiasm for the result. Eloquence may set fire to reason. But whatever may be thought of the redundant discourse before us it had no chance of starting a present conflagration. *If in the long run the beliefs expressed in proletarian dictatorship are destined to be accepted by the dominant forces of the community*, the only meaning of free speech is that they should be given their chance and have their way. [My emphasis.]

Thus, Holmes and Brandeis, too, subscribed to their colleagues' belief that the Due Process Clause of the Fourteenth Amendment "incorporated" the free speech guarantee of the First Amendment, and that state action allegedly violating "due process" could be examined *substantively* by the personal value-laden judicial power of the Supreme Court to ascertain whether the law under attack was constitutionally acceptable by whatever standard at least five justices saw fit to apply.

During the ensuing years, "incorporation" of virtually all other provisions of the Bill of Rights has occurred, violating life, liberty, individual rights, limited government, capitalism, federalism, separation of powers, the appropriate scope of judicial review, and erasing the difference between the explicit provisions of the Bill of Rights and the often amorphous, and formerly procedural, Due Process Clause of the Fourteenth Amendment.

The Constitution of the United States of America had been morphed into a "Living Constitution.

A dozen years after *Gitlow*, the Supreme Court ruled on the 1937 case of *Palko* v. *Connecticut*.[25]

Connecticut had enacted a statute allowing the government to appeal the jury verdict in a criminal case. Palko had been indicted for unpremeditated *second-degree murder*. Convicted, he appealed. The Connecticut Supreme Court reversed and ordered a new trial.

The second time around, Palko was convicted of *first-degree murder* and sentenced to death.

He appealed again, and eventually his case reached the Supreme Court of the United States.

Palko argued that his second trial and conviction violated the Double Jeopardy Clause of the federal *Fifth* Amendment. *Fifth Amendment?* But that applies only to action by the *federal* government. Doesn't it?

Maybe, maybe not.

The question for the Supreme Court was whether Palko's second conviction violated the protection against federal double jeopardy guaranteed by the Fifth Amendment *because this protection, or something like it, applies to the states by virtue of the Fourteenth Amendment's "substantive" Due Process Clause.*

Justice Benjamin Cardozo, for the eight-justice Supreme Court majority, wrote that

> the due process clause of the Fourteenth Amendment may make it unlawful for a State to abridge by its statutes the freedom of *speech* which the First Amendment safeguards against encroachment by the Congress ... or the like freedom of the *press* ... or the free exercise of *religion* ... or the right of peaceable *assembly*, without

which speech would be unduly trammeled ... or the right of one accused of crime to the benefit of *counsel*... . In these and other situations immunities that are valid as against the federal government by force of the specific pledges of particular amendments have been found to be *implicit in the concept of ordered liberty*, and thus, through the Fourteenth Amendment, become valid as against the States. [My emphasis.]

Cardozo was offering his Court and subsequent ones a Bill of Rights menu from which it could pick and choose which federal constitutional provisions could be incorporated into the Fourteenth, and through its Due Process Clause then test the substance of Connecticut's homicide law. Or any state law.

"Ordered liberty"?

Cardozo elaborated: *"A scheme of ordered liberty. A principle of justice so rooted in the traditions and conscience of our people as to be ranked as fundamental."* [My emphasis.]

"Justice"?

"Rooted"?

"Traditions" and "conscience"?

"Fundamental"?

What is meant by "justice ... rooted"?

How does a Supreme Court justice ascertain the "traditions and conscience of our people"?

And whatever those are, and however determined, which of them are "fundamental" and how do we know they are?

These Cardozo-inspired questions sound like Winston Churchill's observation about Soviet Russia as a "riddle wrapped in a mystery inside an enigma."

Cardozo's opinion is utter mumbo jumbo. "Ordered liberty" is

43

worse than no test at all because it provides all courts, and especially the Supreme Court of the United States, with a roving commission to translate the policy values of unelected and unaccountable philosopher kings/queens into what is supposed to pass for constitutional law. *Overriding the states' voters. Overriding governors. Overriding state legislatures.* That our republican system of government and individual rights should rest on such indefensible clichés is blasphemous.

The Supreme Court upheld Palko's second conviction for first-degree murder and death sentence.

In his majority opinion, Cardozo formulated principles that were to inform the Court's substantive due process decisions for the following decades. He noted that some Bill of Rights guarantees—such as freedom of thought and speech—are "fundamental," and that the Fourteenth Amendment's due process clause absorbed those fundamental rights and applied them to the states. Protection against double jeopardy was not a "fundamental" right. At least not for the moment.

But wait.

Isn't the Constitution a Living Document?

Sometimes.

As to Mr. Palko, some thirty years later, in *Benton* v. *Maryland*,[26] Cardozo's successors expressly overruled its decision in *Palko* and incorporated the Double Jeopardy Clause of the Fifth Amendment into the Fourteenth Amendment. However, though now the prohibition on double jeopardy was a "fundamental" right, it did not help Mr. Palko. He died in Connecticut's electric chair on April 12, 1938.

As Professor Raoul Berger explained, "As in the case of the Chinese mandate from heaven, we learn a right is fundamental only after the Court attaches that label. Ordered liberty is too vague to describe a national objective. It says that order and liberty are both to be sought but provides no standard for reconciling the eternal conflict between them. * * * *It is a vehicle for whatever meaning the Court gives it, and thus enables the Court to apply its own conceptions of public policy.*" [My emphasis.]

There is no need to take Professor Berger's word for it. The highly respected Supreme Court Associate Justice Byron White once observed that "ordered liberty" is "[n]o more than a means whereby a majority of the Court [five justices] can impose its own philosophical predilections upon [policy values of] State legislatures or Congress."

With this background, we now stand on the threshold of Chapter 13, deconstructing Washington v. *Glucksberg. There, we will see from the unanimous Supreme Court why Americans do not have the fundamental constitutional right to die.*

To best understand that deconstruction, it will be useful to examine a more recent Fourteenth Amendment, substantive due process, incorporation decision. And, after that, the so-called "privacy" line of cases: *Poe, Griswold, Roe,* and *Casey*.[27]

Timbs v. *Indiana*[28] was a 2019 unanimous decision of the Supreme Court. Let's see what provision of the Bill of Rights was incorporated via the Fourteenth Amendment, what substantive due process tests were applied, and upon what rationales the Supreme Court rested its decision-opinion.

The question before the Court in *Timbs* was whether the federal Eighth Amendment's Excessive Fines Clause—"Excessive bail shall not be required, nor excessive fines imposed"—is an "incorporated" protection applicable to the states through the Fourteenth Amendment's Due Process Clause.

For the Court's majority, Justice Ginsburg wrote:

> Like the Eighth Amendment's proscriptions of 'cruel and unusual punishment' and '[e]xcessive bail,' the protection against excessive fines guards against abuses of government's punitive or criminal-law-enforcement

authority. This safeguard, we hold, is *fundamental to our scheme of ordered liberty,*' with '*dee[p] root[s] in [our] history and tradition.*'" [Sound familiar?] * * * The Excessive Fines Clause is *therefore* incorporated by the *Due Process Clause* of the Fourteenth Amendment." [My emphasis.]

A quadruple-header: "ordered liberty," "deep roots," "history," and "traditions," all in one sentence.

All the fodder for more incremental growth of the Living Constitutional were present: The federal Eighth Amendment's constitutional right of no excessive fines, the Fourteenth Amendment's Due Process Clause, the Substantive Due Process invention, and the baseless Incorporation Doctrine.

Also present were the ambiguous "tests," which the Court found were satisfied: "Ordered liberty," "deep roots," "history," and "traditions."

It is crucial to understand this. The no-right-to-die Supreme Court decision in *Washington* v. *Glucksberg* rests entirely on the same rotten foundation as *Gitlow, Palko, Timbs, and other Supreme Court indefensible decisions*: An explicit federal constitutional right, Due Process of the Fourteenth Amendment, Substantive Due Process, Incorporation, and the Ordered Liberty-Deep Roots-History-Tradition tests. If that foundation is flawed, those decisions, *on that basis alone,* are flawed, bad law. Let alone bad constitutional law.

Let's see if anyone thought that foundation was flawed, and why.

Justice Thomas concurred in the *Timbs* result but wrote a separate concurring opinion. He rightly eschewed the Due Process analysis that was at the foundation of not only the *Timbs* "excessive fines" result, but all of those beginning with the first incorporation in the *Gitlow* case.

> I agree with the Court that the Fourteenth Amendment makes the Eighth Amendment's prohibition on excessive

fines fully applicable to the States. *But I cannot agree with the route the Court takes to reach this conclusion. Instead of reading the Fourteenth Amendment's Due Process Clause to encompass a substantive right that has nothing to do with "process," I would hold that the right to be free from excessive fines is one of the "privileges or immunities of citizens of the United States"* [which is textually] *protected by the Fourteenth Amendment.*

The Fourteenth Amendment provides that "[n]o State shall make or enforce any law which shall abridge the privileges or immunities of citizens of the United States." On its face, this appears to grant ... United States citizens a certain collection of rights—i.e., privileges or immunities—attributable to that status." [29] But as I have previously explained, this Court "marginalized" the Privileges or Immunities Clause in the late 19th century by defining the collection of rights covered by the Clause "quite narrowly." Litigants seeking federal protection of substantive rights against the States thus needed "an alternative fount of such rights," and this Court *"found one in a most curious place,"*—the Fourteenth Amendment's Due Process Clause, which prohibits "any State" from "depriving any person of life, liberty, or property, without due process of law."

Because *this Clause speaks only to "process," the Court has "long struggled to define"* what substantive rights it protects. The Court ordinarily says, as it does today, that the Clause protects rights that are *"fundamental."* Sometimes that means rights that are *"deeply rooted in this Nation's history and tradition."* Other times, when that formulation proves too restrictive, *the Court defines the universe of "fundamental" rights so broadly as to border on meaningless.* See, e.g., Obergefell v. Hodges ... ("rights that allow persons, within a lawful realm, to *define and express their identity*"); Planned Parenthood of Southeastern Pa. v. Casey ... ("At the heart of liberty is the right to *define one's own concept of existence, of meaning, of the universe, and of the mystery of human life"*).

Because the oxymoronic "substantive" "due process" doctrine has no basis in the Constitution, it is unsurprising that the Court has been unable to adhere to any "guiding principle to distinguish 'fundamental' rights that warrant protection from nonfundamental rights that do not."

And because *the Court's substantive due process precedents allow the Court to fashion fundamental rights without any textual constraints*, it is equally unsurprising that among these precedents are some of the *Court's most notoriously incorrect decisions*. E.g., Roe v. Wade; Dred Scott v. Sandford. The present case illustrates the incongruity of the Court's due process approach to incorporating fundamental rights against the States.

Petitioner [Timbs] argues that the forfeiture of his vehicle is an excessive punishment. He does not argue that the Indiana courts failed to proceed according to the "law of the land"—that is, according to written constitutional and statutory provisions, or that the state failed to provide "some baseline procedures." *His claim has nothing to do with any "process" "due" him. I therefore decline to apply the "legal fiction" of substantive due process.* [My emphasis throughout, except for the Dred Scott and Roe mentions which are in the original, and the bracketed material, which is mine.]

Bravo!

If the doctrine of substantive due process, the heart of the "Living Constitution's" desecration of the Declaration of Independence and Constitution, is a legal fiction as Justice Thomas has correctly argued for years, perhaps that explains why Griswold v.

Connecticut, Roe v. Wade and *Planned Parenthood v. Casey, did not rely on that part of the Constitution's anatomy.*

I will explain that presently, but first let's look at what one of the leading Living Constitutionalists has said.

In 1985, then Attorney General of the United States Edwin Meese III delivered a groundbreaking speech to the American Bar Association. In part he said:

> In recent decades many have come to view the Constitution, more accurately part of the Constitution, provisions of the Bill of Rights, the 14th Amendment, as a charter for judicial activism on behalf of various constituencies. Those who hold this view often have lacked demonstrable, textual, or historical support for their conclusions. Instead they have "grounded" their rulings in *appeals to social theories, to model philosophies or personal notions of human dignity, or to "penumbras* somehow emanating ghostlike from various provisions identified—and not identified—in the Bill of Rights. [My emphasis.]

Meese was of course referring to the liberal justices of the Supreme Court and their cohort in academia and the legal profession, all of whom worship at the altar of the "Living Constitution," the High Priest of which was the late, unlamented by Conservatives and Libertarians, Associate Justice William J. Brennan, Jr.

The Constitution, according to Brennan,

> embodies the aspiration to *social justice, brotherhood, and human dignity* that brought this nation into being."
> * * * Our amended Constitution is *the lodestar for our aspirations*, like every text worth reading, it is not crystalline. The phrasing is broad and the limitations of its provisions are not clearly marked. Its *majestic generalities* and *ennobling pronouncement* are both

> luminous and obscure. * * * When justices interpret the Constitution they speak for their *community*, not for themselves alone. The act of interpretation must be undertaken with full consciousness that it is ... the *community's interpretation* that is sought. [My emphasis.]

Putting aside Brennan's flowery, meaningless prose—e.g., "social justice, brotherhood, and human dignity," "crystalline"—his statement is a naked paean to altruism, collectivism, and statism. Brennan sees judges of lower courts and justices of the Supreme Court somehow channeling the "community"—meaning some unidentified and unidentifiable "others"—in ruling on fundamental questions of individual rights. According to Brennan, judges and justices do not decide what the Constitution means. Their friends and neighbors do.

Brennan continued: *"But the ultimate question must be, what do the words or the text mean in our time?"* [My emphasis.]

This revealing sentence by Brennan is a flat-out repudiation of the truism that words have objective meaning. If they do not, words are susceptible to subjective use by any Tom, Dick, or Harry (or William J.) who wants to distort them to serve his own purposes. Brennan's statement is an utter betrayal of the fact that the Constitution means what the Founders wanted it to mean.

Brennan concluded with this paen to the Living Constitution:

> For the genius of the Constitution rests *not in any static meaning* it might have had in *a world that is dead and gone*, but in the adaptability of its great principles to cope with current problems and current *needs*. * * * Our constitution was not intended to preserve a preexisting society, but *to make a new one, to put in place new principles that the prior political community have [sic] not sufficiently recognized.* [My emphasis.]

A "world that is dead and gone," according to Brennan, was the America that proudly declared that "all men are created equal, that they are endowed by their Creator with certain unalienable Rights, that among these are Life, Liberty and the Pursuit of Happiness—That to secure these rights, Governments are instituted among Men, deriving their just powers from the consent of the governed."

Brennan's dead-and-gone world was the one in which American patriots stood at Bunker Hill, Lexington, Concord, and Valley Forge, and at immeasurable cost in blood and treasure eventually threw off the yoke of British tyranny.

A dead-and-gone world whose Constitution promised to "establish Justice" and "secure the Blessings of Liberty."

A dead-and-gone world where the Bill of Rights explicitly rejected the sacrifice of the one to the many and protected individual rights against the collective and its enforcer, a statist government.

A dead-and-gone world in which at least 400,000 men died to vanquish slavery.

A dead-and gone world where Americans shed blood for others at Belleau-Wood, Anzio, Guadalcanal, Chosin, Falluja and places whose names we will never know.

All this was Brennan's "world that is dead and gone," to be replaced by a world conceived by altruists, collectivists, and statists, born in legislatures, and nurtured by courts, a world where "current problems unsolved and current needs" are to be solved and satisfied by the statist power of government.

Brennan and his earlier and later judicial allies corrupted our Constitution in order to repudiate our "preexisting society ... [and] make a new one, to put in place new principles that the prior political community have not sufficiently recognized." *Brennan was saying that the dead hand of the Founders cannot be allowed to leave today's problems unsolved and their needs unsatisfied, no matter how twisted and irrational modern judicial decisions must be in furtherance of that goal.*

That is the constitutional methodology of the altruists, collectivists, and statists, worshiping the religion of the Living Constitution, one fostered in modern times by Justice Brennan and his allies as they looked back with admiration at earlier justices like themselves and politicians such as Woodrow Wilson, Theodore Roosevelt, and Franklin Delano Roosevelt.

That Living Constitution, central to liberal-progressive jurisprudence and palpably evident in Supreme Court adjudication, means no Constitution at all. Because if that methodology is what judges and justices can employ in doing their job, the Constitution is no different from any piece of legislation, which can be constantly amended or repealed every day.

7.

POE V. ULLMAN: BIRTH OF *GRISWOLD V. CONNECTICUT*

Poe v. *Ullman*,[30] a 5-4 decision of the Supreme Court, involved a Fourteenth Amendment Due Process Clause challenge to a Connecticut law that prohibited "the use of contraceptive devices."

The threshold question for the Supreme Court was whether the case as brought was "justiciable." In other words, whether it was within the Court's jurisdiction.

Justice Brennan's reluctant concurring opinion said:

> I agree that this appeal must be dismissed for [plaintiffs'] failure to present a real and substantial controversy which unequivocally calls for adjudication of the rights claimed in advance of any attempt by the State to curtail them by criminal prosecution. * * * It will be time enough to decide the constitutional questions urged upon us when, if ever, that real controversy flares up again. Until it does, or until the State makes a definite and concrete effort to enforce these laws against individual married couples—a threat which it has never made in the past except under the provocation of litigation—this Court may not be compelled to exercise its most delicate power of constitutional adjudication.

Among the four *dissents*, Justice Harlan began by explaining in the more than ten pages of his opinion:

> I am compelled, with all respect, to dissent from the dismissal of these appeals. In my view the course which the Court has taken does violence to established concepts of "justiciability," and unjustifiably leaves these [plaintiffs-] appellants under the threat of unconstitutional prosecution. Regrettably, an adequate exposition of my views calls for a dissenting opinion of unusual length." [My bracketed word.]

Why did Harlan write a dissenting opinion of "unusual length," one might wonder? A cynical observer might conclude that Harlan knew that the real party in interest—Planned Parenthood—would sooner or later be back to the Court with plaintiffs who *had* pleaded proper justiciable allegations, and in his *Poe* dissent Justice Harlan would later have provided the majority ruling that the Connecticut statute was unconstitutional.

The following quotations alone from Justice Harlan's *Poe* dissent convey the flavor for the next Connecticut contraceptive case's majority opinion (to be written by Justice Douglas).

- "Due process has not been reduced to any formula; *its content cannot be determined* by reference to any code." Anything goes. [My emphasis.]

- "[T]he very inclusion of the category of *morality* among state concerns indicates that *society* is not limited in its objects only to the *physical* well-being of the community but traditionally concerned itself with *the moral soundness of its people* as well. Indeed, to attempt a line between public behavior and that which is purely consensual, or solitary would be to withdraw from *community concerns* a range of subjects which with every society in civilized times has found it necessary to deal. [My emphasis.]

The table was now set for *Griswold*, *Roe*, and *Casey*.

8.

GRISWOLD V. CONNECTICUT: PRELUDE TO *ROE* V. *WADE*

Griswold v. Connecticut,[31] whose majority opinion was inspired by *Poe's* dissents, especially Harlan's, is a paradigmatic Living Constitution case, but with a twist. *Griswold* is Constitutional Law 101. It has everything: federalism; separation of powers; judicial review; distortion of the Bill of Rights; substantive due process; incorporation; and a Supreme Court invented, textually non-existent "fundamental right." Also, as usual, it rests on the ideological foundation of altruism, collectivism, and statism.

The majority and concurring opinions in *Griswold* employ a method of constitutional legerdemain which, like sausage-making, is not pretty to watch.

The same Connecticut statute that was involved in *Poe* provided that "[a]ny person who uses any drug, medicinal article or instrument for the purpose of preventing conception shall be fined not less than fifty dollars or imprisoned not less than sixty days nor more than a year or be both fined and imprisoned."[32]

Another section provided that "[a]ny person who assists, abets, counsels, causes, hires or commands another to commit any offense may be prosecuted and punished as if he were the principal offender."

It is important to recognize that the Connecticut law was the product of democratic processes and had been in place since the 1800s. Back in the day, qualified Connecticut voters elected the legislature. The legislature, with quorums present and on majority votes, enacted the law. The governor approved it. Democracy in action! But unacceptable to the Living Constitutionalists, altruists, collectivists, and statists.

The Tenth Amendment has long been recognized as granting the states power to pass laws relating to the public health, welfare, public safety, and, yes, even morals. It was pursuant to that police power that Connecticut enacted the anti-contraceptive law.[33]

But where in the federal Constitution was there a provision saying the *State of* Connecticut could not pass an anti-contraception law? And where was it written that a *federal court* could strike down the action of the Connecticut *voters, state legislature, and governor*?

Because the *federal* Constitution does not prohibit the states from enacting outrageous laws, the Court had to find some way to hold the Connecticut statute unconstitutional. Chief Justice Earl Warren assigned the task to Associate Justice William O. Douglas, a darling of America's liberals and progressives.

In a barely three-page, tossed-off opinion likely written by one of his clerks and, at best, edited by Douglas, the notorious Living Constitutionalist prospected his way through the Bill of Rights. Although what he found was fool's gold, it glittered enough to satisfy six of his colleagues.

According to Douglas, prior cases of the Supreme Court "suggested that specific guarantees in the Bill of Rights"—dealing with speech, press, association, search and seizure, self-incrimination, and the education of one's children—"have *penumbras*,[34] formed by *emanations*[35] from those guarantees that help give them life and substance." [My emphasis.]

8. Griswold v. Connecticut: Prelude to Roe v. Wade

In translation, Douglas and six of his majority colleagues were saying that earlier *language* in Bill of Rights cases sent out *signals*—note he did not say actual case "holdings, "rulings," or "decisions"—which shed negative light on Connecticut's anti-contraceptive law. Note that this mumbo jumbo opinion did not cite a single previous Supreme Court precedent to support the constitutional con that Douglas was running.

Not one.

Based on these emanation-producing penumbras only, about which the liberal Warren Court majority failed to produce a shred of legal, let alone constitutional, precedent or other legal authority, the Court simply invented a constitutionally guaranteed "right of privacy." Without even a nod to how the *federal* Supreme *Court* of the United States had the power to ride roughshod over a *state* statute enacted by its voter-elected *legislature* and approved by its *governor*.

For the seven-justice majority, Douglas wrote:

> We deal with a right of privacy older than the Bill of Rights [What preexisting "right of privacy" was that?]—older than our political parties, older than our school system. Marriage [about which the Connecticut law said nothing] is a coming together for better or for worse, hopefully enduring, and intimate to the degree of being sacred [said the four-times married, thrice divorced justice]. It is an association that promotes a way of life, not causes; a harmony in living, not political faiths; a bilateral loyalty, not commercial or social projects. Yet it is an association for as noble a purpose as any involved in our prior decisions. [My bracketed material.]

Despite this pretentious, contentless mumbo jumbo, or perhaps because of it, neither Douglas nor any of his six colleagues had an answer to a simple question asked in Associate Justice Potter Stewart's dissent, in which Justice Hugo Black joined. Returning to basics, Stewart asked:

> *What provision of the Constitution ... make[s] this State law invalid?* The Court says it is the right of privacy "created by several fundamental constitutional guarantees." With all deference, I can find no such general right of privacy in the Bill of Rights, in any other part of the Constitution, or in any case ever before decided by this Court. [My emphasis.]

To the contrary, despite the clarity of Stewart's unanswerable dissent—and because the seven-justice Warren Court majority and its allies wanted to rid Connecticut of what Stewart rightly characterized as an "uncommonly silly law"—the *Griswold* majority simply invented an ersatz "right to privacy." This anti-federalism, anti-democratic, anti-constitutional judicial invention would later be used by the Court in *Roe* v. *Wade* as foundational precedent to support its invalidating the anti-abortion laws of every state in America all at once.

Consider: This so-called "right to privacy" was a "fundamental right, but as we shall soon see self-termination was not.

As incoherent as was Douglas's stream-of-consciousness majority opinion, the concurring opinion of Justices Arthur Goldberg, William Brennan, and Chief Justice Earl Warren was only slightly more coherent. Agreeing with Douglas that the Connecticut law was unconstitutional, they disagreed with his reasons, unwilling to swallow his amorphous, undefined, ephemeral, emanation/penumbra-driven "right of privacy," which had been suddenly discovered in the Bill of Rights after nearly two centuries.

The concurring trio's rationale for the Court's nullification of the Connecticut anti-contraception law was instead based on their amorphous, undefined concept of something called a "fundamental right" (i.e., purchasing and using contraceptives!), a "right" apparently as "fundamental" as the right to vote, to freely exercise religion and criticize the government.

The willingness of the three concurring justices to thwart the will of Connecticut voters, legislators, and governor was indefensible enough. Worse, by far, were the altruist-collectivist premises Goldberg, Warren, and Brennan revealed in the process—ironically, the very same premises that caused the law's enactment in the first place. Wrote Goldberg:

> In determining which rights are fundamental, judges are not left at large to decide cases in light of *their* personal and private notions. Rather, they must look to the "*traditions* and [collective] *conscience* of our people" to determine whether a principle is "so rooted [there] * * * as to be ranked as fundamental." [My emphasis.]

A modest disclaimer. But while confessing that a *judge's* policy values are not the test by which "fundamental rights" are revealed, Goldberg openly deferred to "the traditions and [collective] conscience of our people"—*a naked admission that rights are neither absolute, nor recognized by and anchored in the Constitution*. According to him, rights are what *society* (i.e., other people) decide. Goldberg and his two altruist-collectivist-statist colleagues further exposed themselves as Living Constitutionalists by their view of what Connecticut society had already decided in related aspects of sexual conduct:

> The State of Connecticut does have statutes, the constitutionality of which is beyond doubt, *which prohibit adultery and fornication*. [My emphasis.]

* * *

> Finally, it should be said of the Court's holding today that it in no way interferes with *a State's proper regulation of sexual promiscuity or misconduct*. [My emphasis.]

Living constitutionalists Goldberg, Warren, and Brennan were, of course, motivated by dogmas about as controllable as a loose cannon on a rolling deck. How else to explain why they *denied* Connecticut the power to interfere with the use of contraceptives, while simultaneously *granting* the state the power to interfere with adultery, fornication, sexual promiscuity, and "misconduct"? Whose interests were being sacrificed, to whom, and why? And who were the enforcers?

When reading *Griswold's* majority and concurring opinions, it is apparent that lurking in the background, unrevealed, is the only existing constitutional doctrine that would have been at least plausible to use against the Connecticut law: *substantive due process of the Fourteenth Amendment.*

But if so, why was it not invoked by at least one of the seven majority justices instead of their signing on to the laughable "right of privacy" invention, while being stuck with the hypocritical contradiction of Connecticut being able to legislate against adultery, fornication, sexual promiscuity, and other conduct more bothersome to the public than the purchase and use of contraceptives?

The answer is revealing.

The majority-concurring justices could not rely on substantive due process because it was a constitutionally meaningless concept, a fiction as Justice Thomas wrote, and they had to know it.

Even they could not have shown that buying and using contraceptives was an essential element of American "ordered liberty," "deeply rooted in the traditions and collective conscience of our people," a right allowing the purchasers and users of contraceptives "to define and express their identity," and a right "to define one's own concept of existence, of meaning, of the universe, and of the mystery of human life?" They would have been—and surely should have been—held up to public ridicule and disgrace.

Obloquy.

Over contraceptives?!

Could seven Supreme Court justices prove constitutionally that the purchase and use of contraceptives was as "fundamental" a right comparable to free exercise of religion, speech, press, assembly, petition, bearing arms, probable cause for warrants, double jeopardy, self-incrimination, due process, eminent domain, impartial jury, confrontation by witnesses, compulsory process and right to counsel?

What about prohibition of excessive bail and fines, cruel and unusual punishment? What about voting?

Contraceptives?!

Recall what Justice Thomas wrote in *Timbs*:

> Because *this Clause speaks only to "process,"* the Court has "long struggled to define" what substantive rights it protects. The Court ordinarily says, as it does today, that the Clause protects rights that are "fundamental." Sometimes that means rights that are "'deeply rooted in this Nation's history and tradition.'" Other times, when that formulation proves too restrictive, *the Court defines the universe of "fundamental" rights so broadly as to border on meaningless.* See, e.g., Obergefell v. Hodges ... ("rights that allow persons, within a lawful realm, to define and express their identity"); Planned Parenthood of Southeastern Pa. v. Casey ... ("At the heart of liberty is the right to define one's own concept of existence, of meaning, of the universe, and of the mystery of human life").
>
> *Because the oxymoronic "substantive" "due process" doctrine has no basis in the Constitution, it is unsurprising that the Court has been unable to adhere to any "guiding principle to distinguish 'fundamental' rights that warrant protection from nonfundamental rights that do not."* [My emphasis throughout.]

But Justice Thomas's dissent in *Timbs* is not the end of the story *Griswold* teaches us.

Even worse than the Court's invalidating Connecticut's law, *the*

Griswold majority endorsed, albeit implicitly, a forced-sterilization program—even for married couples:

> [T]he Government, *absent a showing of a compelling subordinate State interest*, could not decree that all husbands and wives must be sterilized after two children have been born to them. [My emphasis.]

That's right. *Absent a showing*.

Please read that sentence again carefully. If such "a showing of a compelling subordinate State interest" *was* made*, then the statist government could "decree that all husbands and wives must be sterilized after two children have been born to them."*

You read it right.

What if there was a "showing?"

Then, Americans' desire for a third or more child would be sacrificed—literally sacrificed! — to a "compelling subordinate State [i.e., collectivist] interest." Just as in Communist China, socialist India, and other statist regimes.

So much for "fundamental rights." Let alone other rights of lesser importance.

Justice John Marshall Harlan's concurring opinion in *Griswold* was cast from the same mold as his fellow justices' opinions and his earlier dissent in *Poe* v. *Ullman*. However, Harlan's constitutional "test" was neither the majority's "right of privacy" nor the Goldberg concurring "fundamental rights," two hollow Living Constitutionalist slogans more suitable for a political speech than a Supreme Court opinion.

Instead, Harlan's concurring opinion placed his constitutional chips on "basic values implicit in the concept of ordered liberty." That, in Harlan's view, is what justified the Court's invalidation of Connecticut's democratically enacted anti-contraception law.

8. Griswold v. Connecticut: Prelude to Roe v. Wade

What he meant by "ordered liberty" is explained by what he had written earlier in *Poe*:[36]

> I would not suggest that adultery, homosexuality, fornication, and incest are immune from criminal enquiry, however privately practiced. So much has been explicitly recognized in acknowledging the State's rightful concern for *its people's moral welfare*. [My emphasis.]

Thus, in Harlan's view, society (lots of people) can criminalize certain sexual practices, subordinating the preferences of the practitioners to the collective's judgment of what is "moral," and enforced by the coercive power of the state.

Why, then, should Connecticut "society" not be able to criminalize the purchase and use of contraceptives?

In what way does Connecticut's criminalization not foster "the State's rightful concern for its people's moral welfare," about which Harlan is so solicitous? His answer:

> Adultery, homosexuality and the like are sexual intimacies which the State [lots of other people] forbids altogether, but the intimacy of husband and wife is necessarily an *essential and accepted feature of the institution of marriage, an institution which the State not only must allow, but which always and in every age it has fostered and protected.* It is one thing when the State exerts its power either to forbid extra-marital sexuality altogether, or to say who may marry, but it is quite another when, having acknowledged a marriage and the intimacies inherent in it, it undertakes to *regulate by means of the criminal law* the details of that intimacy. [My emphasis.]

> Requiring husband and wife to render account before a criminal tribunal of their uses of that intimacy, is surely a different thing indeed from punishing those who establish intimacies which the law has always forbidden and *which can have no claim to social protection.* [My emphasis.]

Justice Harlan never told anyone why it is "surely a different thing."

If we blend Harlan's *Poe* dissent, Douglas's *Griswold* majority opinion, the Goldberg-Warren-Brennan and Harlan concurring opinion, the result is this: "Society" (one's friends and neighbors, and even strangers) on moral and other grounds has a legitimate interest in marriage and sex. Thus, society, acting through government, can criminalize the sexual conduct of some of its members, but because of "tradition" and a "government interest" in marriage cannot go so far as to prohibit the use of contraceptives by married heterosexuals.

According to Douglas and the others who joined his indefensible *Griswold* majority opinion, "emanations" and "penumbras" in virtually every provision of the Bill of Rights create a constitutional "right of privacy".

According to the concurring Griswold opinions, the Connecticut contraception "right" is "fundamental," gleaned from the "*traditions* and [collective] *conscience* of our people" and elsewhere. This sentiment was joined by Harlan, because in the name of morality society traditionally approves of certain sexual acts and their practitioners while it disapproves of others.

We have not seen the last of *Griswold* v. *Connecticut*. I will revisit it later, where it will become clear how its methodology and status as precedent enabled the Court to explode the growth of the Living Constitution.

A Living Constitution is not only an anti-democratic and intellectually dishonest way to interpret our Constitution and federal statutes, but also demonstrably capable of inventing dangerous ersatz "rights"—such as *Griswold*'s spurious "right of privacy"—which impose tremendous moral, legal, social, economic, political, and other costs on this nation and its citizens.

Griswold's interpretive methodology—imposed on the basic Constitution, on the Bill of Rights, on the Fourteenth Amendment, and on federal statutes—and the invention and institutionalization of ersatz "rights" has made possible the decades-long metastasis of the Living Constitution's malignant anti-federalism and its anti–separation of powers doctrines into most areas of American constitutional and statutory law.

All of this leaves us with one more question: What has been incorporated? The answer: virtually every provision of the Bill of Rights.

Not only have they been incorporated, "emanations" and "penumbras" from specific Bill of Rights provisions have created another non-textual "right" that the Founders in their wildest dreams could not have imagined. An anti textual "right" that is at the top of the "worst of the worst" Supreme Court cases ever decided.

Which brings us back to *Griswold*'s progeny, the infamous stain on nearly two hundred years of Supreme Court decisions, *Roe v. Wade*,[37] which together with *Dred Scott* reeks with arrogant unconstitutionality and immoral inhumanity.

9.

ROE V. *WADE*: OVERTURE TO *COMPASSION IN DYING* V. *WASHINGTON*

My earlier discussion of *Griswold* leaves no doubt that far from being a victory for contraceptive purchasers' and users' "choice," the decision—rooted as it was in constitutional doubletalk, altruism-collectivism-statism, and disregard of federalism, separation of powers, and judicial restraint—exemplifies Living Constitutionalism at its worst and most dangerous.

Dangerous because Justice Douglas's ersatz "right to privacy" would, eight years later, be utilized by the Supreme Court in *Roe* v. *Wade* to justify invalidating every state law regulating abortion. And in so doing, legalize and constitutionalize the killing of countless millions of the unborn.

A Texas statute, like those in many of the states in the early 1970s, had outlawed abortion except to save the mother's life.

Jane Roe (a pseudonym)—unmarried, pregnant, and a pawn of pro-abortion zealots—sued in a federal court to declare the Texas anti-abortion statute unconstitutional.

Relying principally on *Griswold*'s "right of privacy, the Fourteenth Amendment's substantive due process "tests" and the

Incorporation Doctrine, Ms. Roe claimed the statute violated her rights of personal "privacy" and "liberty." She cited no other source, constitutional or otherwise, to justify her alleged right to an abortion and destruction of the baby she was carrying.

The Supreme Court's decision in *Roe* was, to be charitable, fragmented—even more than *Griswold* had been. Of the nine justices in *Roe*, six wrote separate opinions. The majority opinion was written by Justice Harry Blackmun and concurred in by Chief Justice Warren Burger, Justices William O. Douglas, William J. Brennan, Potter Stewart, Thurgood Marshall, and Lewis Powell. Three of the concurring justices—Burger, Douglas, and Stewart—wrote individual opinions. While Justice William Rehnquist joined a dissent by Justice Byron White, Rehnquist wrote a separate dissenting opinion of his own. This was a sure sign—indeed, a confession—that the majority was on thin constitutional ice, creating and trying to justify a *policy* decision instead of a *constitutional* one.

In his majority opinion, Justice Blackmun held the Texas anti-abortion statute unconstitutional.

He reached that conclusion by canvassing a wide variety of sources, seeking to ascertain what their attitudes were toward abortion. As if that had anything to do with whether there was a constitutional "right of privacy" lurking somewhere in the Constitution that would justify as a matter of convenience ripping a baby from a woman's womb.

What sources?

Blackmun examined ancient views, which were not only inconclusive but also irrelevant in an American court.

He claimed that the rigid anti-abortion aspect of the Hippocratic Oath had been "unpopular" at the time it was formulated. By itself, that was no reason to strike down every law in America that dealt with abortion.

He perused English common law, where to support his sought-after conclusion he was seeking he learned that under early English law abortion to save the mother's life was not considered a crime. That did not mean that under the American Constitution and state laws anti-abortion statutes were unconstitutional.

The *Roe* case was about whether the sovereign State of Texas (and thus every other state) had Tenth Amendment police power to enact an anti-abortion statute. If it did, was there *an explicit provision of the Constitution—an explicit federal constitutional right of Ms. Roe—that was violated by such a statute?* English law should have had nothing to do with the answer to those profoundly important American jurisprudential questions.

Blackmun liked British law because he didn't fare as well in his survey of American law. "By the end of the 1950s," he wrote, "a large majority of the jurisdictions [the States, in the United States] banned abortion, however and whenever performed, unless done to save or preserve the life of the mother." Apparently, that was of no importance to Blackmun, who often counted the noses of "society" when that tactic was useful to him.

Summarizing his survey of the irrelevant past, Blackmun observed:

> It is thus apparent that at [English] common law, at the time of the adoption of our Constitution, and throughout the major portion of the 19th century, abortion was *viewed with less disfavor* than under most American statutes currently [1973] in effect. Phrasing it another way, a woman enjoyed a substantially broader right to terminate a pregnancy than she does in most States today. At least with respect to the early stage of pregnancy, and very possibly without such a limitation, the opportunity to make this choice was present in this country well into the 19th century. Even later, the law continued for some time to treat less punitively an abortion procured in early pregnancy.

So what?

These observations, of course, had nothing to do with the Tenth Amendment. Nor federalism, separation of powers, the appropriate scope of judicial review, or the Bill of Rights—except to implicitly and importantly acknowledge that, until *Roe*, legislation on the subject of abortion was, under the Tenth Amendment, exclusively the province of the *states*, whose voters, legislators, governors, and courts apparently never realized that their laws somehow infringed emanating penumbras which phantom-like created an American constitutional "right of privacy."

Next, Blackmun turned his attention to medical views, past and prevailing. Since the mid-nineteenth century, the American Medical Association had bitterly condemned abortion, only to ameliorate its harsh view in the hippie Sixties. In reviewing the American Public Health Association's pro-abortion position, Blackmun noted that just the year before, the American Bar Association had approved a Uniform Abortion Act prepared by the prestigious Conference of Commissioners on Uniform State Laws. Blackmun's potpourri of current views now included legal as well as medical authorities.

It was embarrassingly obvious what Blackmun was trying to cobble together from all this opinion-gathering: *Some kind of historical, cultural, social* (but certainly not constitutional) *consensus justification for abortion.* If, in these respects, abortion had been treated even equivocally, the Court's task—coming up with a favorable abortion ruling—would be easier. Blackmun and his colleagues could write, as it were, on a clean slate. Ironically, but not surprisingly, what he wrote was, in turn, equivocal:

> We, therefore, conclude that the right of personal privacy includes the abortion decision, but that this right is *not unqualified* and must be considered against *important State interests* in regulation. [My emphasis.]

"Important State interests" again. And who, or what, is this "State"? Is it voters, neighbors, relatives, politicians, legislators, judges, bartenders? felons? Who? *The* woman next door?

"State interests" this time would be concerned not with weak, dependent women (*Muller*) or marital sexual conduct (*Griswold*), but the unborn in the wombs of pregnant women. This time, the babies would be the losers to that state interest.

It is difficult to imagine any more naked altruist-collectivist-statist, let alone indefensible non-constitutional, ruling. It was literal sacrifice of millions of the unborn to the norms of the "pro-choice" collectivist left, enforced by the blunt-force statist power of the United States government. By "society."

Roe presented a constitutional case raising fundamental questions of federalism, separation of powers, the scope of judicial review, the Tenth Amendment, and the Bill of Rights. Americans had the right to expect a United States Supreme Court decision and opinion that presented a solid array of legal-constitutional thought and analysis, reinforced with impeccable reasoning and irrefutable logic. We find in *Roe* instead, as sole constitutional justification for its decision, the amorphous, Douglas-invented "right of personal privacy," unintelligibly and unintelligently imported in all its absurdity, indefensibility and judicial arrogance from *Griswold* and from Harlan's earlier *Poe* dissent.

Indeed, even Blackmun had to concede that in *Roe* Douglas's intellectually dishonest right of "privacy" was nowhere to be found in the Constitution.

So, to deal with that deficiency, following Douglas's earlier lead Blackmun tried to weave his own "privacy right" into the Bill of Rights by selecting threads where he could. *Yet Blackmun's entire fifty-four-page opinion—which would in a single decision invalidate anti-abortion laws nationwide, and lead to literally uncountable deaths of the unborn—contained only a single paragraph devoted to the purported constitutional basis for the Court's conclusion*:

> *The Constitution does not explicitly mention any right of privacy.* In a line of decisions, however, going back perhaps as far as ... 1891 ... the Court has *recognized* that

a right of personal privacy, or a guarantee of certain areas or zones of privacy, does exist under the Constitution. In varying contexts, the Court or individual Justices have, indeed, found *at least the roots of that right* in the First Amendment ... in the Fourth and Fifth Amendments ... in the *penumbras* of the Bill of Rights ... in the Ninth Amendment ... *or in the concept of liberty* guaranteed by the first section of the Fourteenth Amendment are deemed "fundamental" or "implicit in the concept of ordered liberty" ... are included in this guarantee of personal privacy. They also make it clear that the right has some extension to activities relating to marriage ... procreation ... contraception ... family relationships ... and child rearing and education.... . [My emphasis.]

This one paragraph explication of a constitutional wish list was the sole excuse during the following half-century for uncountable numbers of babies to die, sacrificed on the altar of altruism, collectivism, and statism, usually for the mother's convenience.

The Court's literally Solomonic policy decision went so far as to give the states a trimester schedule for the killing. Because the Court in 1973 considered abortions within the first trimester to be as medically safe as, or even safer than normal childbirth, abortions in the first three months of pregnancy "must be left to the medical judgment of the pregnant [woman and her] attending physician." This was not constitutional law. It was a compromising *legislative policy decision* masquerading as constitutional adjudication.

Because the Court invoked a state interest in the health of the pregnant woman (see *Muller* v. *Oregon*), abortions during the stage after approximately the end of the first trimester could be regulated "in ways that are reasonably related to maternal health" (e.g., licensed physicians, adequate facilities). More policy.

Because the Court asserted a state interest in what it narrowly considered to be *potential* life (which would be destroyed), "[f] or the stage subsequent to viability [approximately during the final trimester], the State ... may, if it chooses, regulate, and even proscribe, abortion except where it is necessary, in appropriate medical judgment, for the preservation of the life or health of the mother." Note the Court's presumptuous, arrogant disregard of federalism, separation of powers, and judicial restraint by legislating the killing schedule for the fifty states.

Few realized at the time that *Roe* v. *Wade* had opened a Pandora's box. By adopting the essence of *Muller* v. *Oregon,* the Supreme Court cavalierly legitimized a "state interest" in pregnant women and their unborn babies. Although in *Roe* anti-abortion laws were struck down to the loud applause of the "pro-choice" zealots, they should not have rejoiced. Not only because of the barbaric consequences of that decision, but also because of its horrendous implications.

In 1973, some women were permitted to have abortions, *sometimes*, if they followed the Supreme Court's trimester killing schedule.

But what about next time, if the "state interest" was a governmental Malthusian need to compel abortions?

Compel abortions? In the United States of America? Kill babies in the womb, despite non-consenting parents?

Science fiction.

Unthinkable.

Not if we accept the inescapable, ultimate logic of *Roe* v. *Wade,* as seen from the perspective of a 1977 Supreme Court case.

The states, in the wake of *Roe* v. *Wade*, were obliged to revise not only their abortion laws but also a considerable number of related laws directly and indirectly affected by that decision. One example was Medicaid, which prior to *Roe* had funded certain *childbearing* expenses.

Connecticut Welfare Department regulations, which paid for *childbirth* expenses, limited State Medicaid benefits for first trimester abortions to those that were "medically necessary." In a 1977 case, *Maher* v. *Roe* [38] (a different Roe), the Supreme Court was asked to decide "whether the Constitution requires a ... State to pay for ... [non-medically necessary] *abortions* when it pays for *childbirth*." [My emphasis.]

In other words, did Connecticut have a constitutional right to have a Medicaid funding policy that financially treated birth and abortion *differently*?

Before answering that question, the Court felt obliged to point out what *Roe* v. *Wade* had *not* held. According to the 1977 *Maher* v. *Roe* decision,

> *Roe* did not declare an unqualified constitutional right to an abortion... . * * * [The decision] implies no limitation on the authority of a State to *make a value judgment favoring childbirth over abortion*, and to implement that judgment by the allocation of public [Medicaid] funds.

In other words, under, or despite, *Roe*, state governments could make "value judgments"— i.e., pass laws—*limiting* abortions.

All well and good. But pro-life people should not have applauded.

If the State could favor *childbirth over abortion*, why could it not favor *abortion over childbirth*?

Compelled abortion!

Absurd?

Think again.

Following the 6–3 majority's statement in *Roe* that "[t]he State unquestionably has a 'strong and legitimate interest in encouraging normal childbirth' ... an interest honored over the centuries," there appeared a footnote *by the Roe majority* as astonishing as it was ominous:

> In addition to the direct interest in protecting the fetus, a State may have *legitimate demographic concerns about its rate of population growth* [or food, or pharmaceutical supplies?]. Such concerns are *basic to the future of the State* and in some circumstances could constitute a substantial reason for *departure from a position of neutrality between abortion and childbirth*. [My emphasis in italics and bracketed material.]

If government is not "neutral," it necessarily tilts to one side or the other. And even if it tilts *for* childbirth and *against* abortion, under the rationales of *Muller, Poe, Griswold, Roe, Maher* and other decisions, it can as quickly and easily tilt *against* childbirth and *for* abortion—not unlike democratic India, whose "demographic concerns about its rate of population growth" some years ago prompted it to depart "from a position of neutrality between abortion and childbirth" by instituting a program of *forced sterilization*. And let us not forget Communist China, whose perceived need for male infants has for generations resulted in state-ordered and state-sanctioned female infanticide.

This frightening *American* Supreme Court story gets worse.

Brennan, Marshall and Blackmun (principal author of *Roe*) dissented in the *Maher* case. One might have expected a ringing denunciation of the majority's ominous assertion that, should population grow too large (or food become too scarce, or a rogue pharmaceutical cause in-womb deformities?), "society" could *forcibly rid itself of the unborn.*

There was no denunciation. Not one word from any of the three liberals.

Why?

Because in the end, albeit regarding different issues and in different degrees, too many judges and too many other Americans are at their core altruists, collectivists, and statists, the only difference being what government conduct they value or disvalue at any given moment.

No one won in *Roe* v. *Wade*. Not Texas, Roe herself, the Court, nor constitutional law. Certainly, during the last fifty-years not the countless aborted unborn who have died because the Living Constitution lives. And grows.

Just as no one had won when procedural due process was morphed into a substantive tool to be used against state legislation, and when virtually every provision of the Bill of Rights was "incorporated" against the states, and the Supreme Court of the United States began to invent non-textual "fundamental" rights to feed the altruist-collectivist-statist appetite for more government control at the expense of individual rights.

The sad, indisputable fact is that Americans do not own their lives, others do.

Accordingly, we do not own the right to die as we see fit.

The same federal case in four courts tells this part of our story.

- *Compassion in Dying* v. *State of Washington*, 850 F.Supp. 1454 (1994). United States District Court for the Western District of Washington at Seattle.

- *Compassion in Dying* v. *State of Washington*, 49 F.3d 586 (1995). United States Court of Appeals, Ninth Circuit.

- *Compassion in Dying* v. *State of Washington*, 79 F.2d 790 (1996), *en banc*.

- *Washington* v. *Glucksberg*, 571 U.S. 702 (1997). Supreme Court of the United States.

10.

COMPASSION IN DYING V. *WASHINGTON*; FEDERAL DISTRICT COURT

Judicial confrontation with the fundamental moral and legal question of the right to die began in a Washington State federal district court.

Doubtless cognizant of the frequent "standing to sue" problem in such public policy "cause" litigation, the lead plaintiff was the Compassion in Dying nonprofit, followed by four licensed physicians and three terminally ill patients.

The plaintiffs sought a declaratory judgment that a Washington statute prohibiting causing or aiding another person to commit suicide violated the Constitution of the United States of America.

The first paragraph of the Chief Judge's opinion reads as follows:

> This court is asked to rule as a matter of first impression on the constitutionality of the State of Washington's *criminal prohibition against physician-assisted suicide.* Specifically, the plaintiffs assert that the Fourteenth Amendment to the United States Constitution guarantees adults who are mentally competent, *terminally ill*, and acting under no undue influence the right to voluntarily

hasten their death by taking a lethal dose of physician-prescribed drugs. Plaintiffs accordingly challenge the constitutionality of [the Washington statute] RCW 9A. 36.060, which makes it a felony to knowingly aid another person in committing suicide. *Plaintiffs challenge the statute only insofar as it bans physician-assisted suicide by mentally competent, terminally ill adults who knowingly and voluntarily choose to hasten their death.* [My emphasis]

I have emphasized the last sentence because it is noteworthy that the plaintiffs were content to argue that the Fourteenth Amendment invalidated only the *physical* (not mental) suffering of *terminal* patients. These were moral and tactical concessions by the plaintiffs that the law's supposed protection could attach conditions to suicide, and that there was no absolute, unconditional right to die or to assist someone else's suicide. (For comments on physician-assisted suicide, see Appendices A and B.)

Moreover, although The State of Washington had no law prohibiting suicide or an attempted suicide that failed, it did ban aiding or causing the suicide of another: "A person is guilty of promoting a suicide attempt when he knowingly causes or aids another person to attempt suicide. * * * Promoting a suicide attempt is a class C *felony* punishable by imprisonment for a maximum of five years and a fine of up to ten thousand dollars." [My emphasis.]

The Chief Judge of The United States District Court for the Western District of Washington agreed with the plaintiffs and granted summary judgment, holding that the statute violated the liberty guaranteed by the Fourteenth Amendment.[39]

In support of that conclusion, Chief Judge Rothstein's legal analysis of why plaintiffs had a protected liberty interest rested on two foundations, each built on two cases previously decided by the Supreme Court of the United States.

First was the "liberty interest" under *Planned Parenthood* v. *Casey*, which I turn to now.

Casey was a bitter 5-4 decision in which the Court reaffirmed *Roe* v. *Wade* , but *Casey* changed an important rule. This time, the justices imposed a new standard that would determine the validity of laws impacting on the practice of abortion. The new standard would ask whether a state abortion regulation had the purpose or effect of imposing an "undue burden" on a pregnant woman seeking to abort her baby—a "substantial obstacle in the path of a woman seeking an abortion before the fetus attains *viability.*" [My emphasis.]

This time around, gone was the trimester killing schedule.

As in *Roe*, there was so much division and perhaps embarrassment on the Court, in a rare occurrence its opinion was team-written and authored by three justices: O'Connor, Kennedy, and Souter (all appointed by Republican presidents.)

In the federal district court, Chief Judge Rothstein acknowledged the "long line of cases" wherein the Supreme Court of the United States had recognized liberty interests in "personal decisions relating to marriage, procreation, contraception, family relationships, child rearing and education." In other words, because the Court had found a liberty interest in the foregoing ("procreation" being code for abortion) a more fundamental interest was the right to self-termination (but inevitably, only under rules established by the state).

According to the Chief Judge,

> The opinion in *Casey* involved a woman's right to choose abortion, and thus did not address the question of what liberty interest may inhere in a terminally ill person's choice to commit suicide. However, this court finds the [Supreme Court's] reasoning highly instructive and almost prescriptive [required] on the latter [suicide] issue. Like the abortion decision, the decision of a

terminally ill person to end his or her life "involve[es] the most intimate and personal choices a person may make in a lifetime" and constitutes "a choice central to personal dignity and autonomy." [Quoting *Casey*.]

Although abortion and suicide were factually different, the Chief Judge saw a single principle uniting the two acts: Making a choice "central to personal dignity and autonomy."

Ironic?

No.

Chief Judge Rothstein was saying that if pursuant to Roe v. Wade a pregnant woman could kill her baby, surely she had a moral and constitutional right to kill herself or, by implication, help someone else commit suicide.

Continuing to rely on *Casey*, Chief Judge Rothstein noted that neither she nor Supreme Court justices possessed the right to impose a particular moral standard on private individuals.

She ruled that the facts of *Compassion in Dying*, and the principle compelling *Casey's* right of abortion, required the same right-to-die result in this case.

Chief Judge Rothstein then turned to the other pillar that supported her conclusion, plaintiffs' "liberty interest under *Cruzan v. Director, Missouri Dept. of Health*,[40] which she found "instructive."

> In Cruzan, the Supreme Court considered whether a competent person has a constitutionally protected liberty interest in refusing unwanted, life-sustaining medical treatment including artificially delivered food and water essential to life. In his majority opinion, Justice Rehnquist acknowledged that this principle "may be inferred from our prior decisions ... and that the logic of the cases ... would embrace such a liberty interest. * * * He then assumed for purposes of the case before the

Court "that the United States Constitution would grant a competent person a constitutionally protected right to refuse lifesaving hydration and nutrition.

If, by now, the reader wonders what the difference is between a woman who wants to die passively by declining life-sustaining treatment and thus deliberately poisoning herself when the body shuts down, so, too, did Chief Judge Rothstein:

> The question [is] whether a constitutional distinction can be drawn between refusal or withdrawal of medical treatment which results in death, and the situation in this case involving competent, terminally ill individuals who wish to hasten death by self-administering drugs prescribed by a physician. *In other words, is there a difference for purposes of finding a Fourteenth Amendment liberty interest between refusal of unwanted treatment which will result in death and committing physician-assisted suicide in the final stage of life?* [My emphasis.]

Finding no difference, and "[b]ased on *Casey* and *Cruzan*," the court conclude[d] "that a competent, terminally ill adult has a constitutionally guaranteed right under the Fourteenth Amendment to commit physician-assisted suicide."

The State of Washington appealed.

11.

COMPASSION IN DYING V. *WASHINGTON*; FEDERAL CIRCUIT COURT

A three-judge panel—Judges Wright, Noonan, and Scannlain—heard the case in the United States Court of Appeals for the Ninth Circuit and reversed the district court.

Judge Noonan wrote the majority opinion for himself and Judge Scannlain. He advanced five reasons for reversing the district court.

First, apparently unwittingly, he invoked a *reductio ad absurdum*.[41] After simply asserting that Chief Judge Rothstein had taken *Casey's* words out of context, Judge Noonan wrote:

> If at the heart of the liberty protected by the Fourteenth Amendment is this uncurtailable ability to believe and act on one's deepest beliefs about life, the right to suicide and the right to assistance in suicide are the prerogative of at least every sane adult. *The attempt to restrict such rights to the terminally ill is illusory.* If such liberty exists in this context, as Casey asserted in the context of reproductive rights, *every man and woman in the United States must enjoy it.* * * * The conclusion is a *reductio ad absurdum*. [My emphasis.]

Yes, absolutely correct!

Recall what I wrote above: *"It is noteworthy that the plaintiffs were content to argue the Fourteenth Amendment invalidated only the physical (not mental) suffering of terminal patients. This was a moral and tactical concession by the plaintiffs that the Amendment's supposed protection could attach conditions, and that there was no absolute, unconditional right to die."*

What Judge Noonan intended as an argument *against* the unqualified right to die is an argument in *favor* of that liberty right, not only for the physical suffering of the terminally ill, but also for anyone who has tired of life, no matter what their reason. We do not live for others except by voluntary choice, let alone for the benefit of the altruists, collectivists, and statists.

Second, Judge Noonan criticized the district court's reliance on *Cruzan* because in that case Justice Rehnquist referred to the state's interest "in the protection and preservation of human life." As I pointed out above, the core point is not *that* the state may have such an interest, but *why* and *in whose name* it does. The chapters above reveal clearly why and whom that is. Thus, Noonan parroted the indefensible principles and justification of government ownership of our lives and deaths, along with concomitant control of our constitutional right to die when, where, why, and how of our own choosing.

Third, he repeated another of the usually invoked but stale justifications by criticizing the district court's opinion for taking account of "the traditions of our nation," a platitude with little or no meaning. He wrote:

> In the two hundred and five years of our existence no constitutional right to aid in killing oneself has ever been asserted and upheld by a court of final jurisdiction. Unless the federal judiciary is to be a floating constitutional convention, a federal court should not invent a constitutional right unknown to the past and

antithetical to the defense of human life that has been a chief responsibility of our constitutional government.

Putting aside that *Compassion in Dying* was the first assisted-suicide case, judicial definition of a liberty interest in the context of self-termination is hardly "a floating constitutional convention." It is simply nine justices doing their job, in a single case.

Finally, where was it written that "the defense of human life ... has been a chief responsibility of our constitutional government"? See, for example, *Dred Scott, Arver* v. *United States* (*Selective Draft Law Cases*), *Buck* v. *Bell, Roe* v. *Wade* and others such as anti-capital punishment death cases that disdained the lives of crime victims.

The several other arguments Judge Noonan used against the district court's decision were based on such considerations as ancient history (e.g., the Hippocratic Oath), public policy (e.g., "protecting minorities from exploitation"), wishful thinking (e.g., medical progress), and strawman appeals (e.g., compassion). Recall what Blackmun had tried to rely on in *Roe*.

It is with a nod to "compassion" that Judge Noonan concluded his failed attempt to repudiate the district court's ruling.

> Compassion is a proper, desirable, even necessary component of judicial character, but compassion is not the most important, certainly not the sole law of human existence. Unrestrained by other virtues ... it leads to catastrophe. Justice, prudence, and fortitude are necessary too. Compassion cannot be the compass of a federal judge. That compass is the Constitution of the United States. Where, as here in the case of Washington, the statute of a state comports with that compass the validity of the statute must be upheld.

If it is the Constitution that points a federal judge to the correct decision about the meaning of Fourteenth Amendment "liberty" in the context of the right to die, Ninth Circuit Judges Noonan and Scannlain went in the wrong direction. As dissenting Judge Wright wrote,

> This case involves the state's power arbitrarily to deprive terminally ill, mentally competent adults of the right to choose how to die. Because [the Washington statute] violates plaintiffs' privacy ... rights, I dissent. The majority's approach subjects such patients to unwanted and needless suffering. * * * The ... patients were terminally ill, mentally competent adults, entitled to be free from unwarranted state interference in their last days.

Tracking the district court's analysis and arguments, Judge Wright concluded by observing that "[t]he right to die with dignity accords with the American values of self-determination and privacy regarding personal decisions."

And, one can add, with the Constitution's Fourteenth Amendment guarantee of liberty.

12.

COMPASSION IN DYING V. *WASHINGTON*; FEDERAL CIRCUIT COURT, *EN BANC*

Having lost 2-1, plaintiffs requested and received a rehearing *en banc*.

Eleven of the Ninth Circuit judges heard the case. Judge Rheinhardt wrote the majority opinion for himself and Judges Browning, Hug, Schroeder, Fletcher, Pregerson, Wigans, and Thompson. Judges Beezer, Fernandez, and Kleinfeld dissented.

The majority and dissenting opinions of the *en banc* bench are approximately eighty pages long and are not useful if read in their entirety. The court began:

> This case raises an extraordinarily important and difficult issue. It compels us to address questions to which there are no easy or simple answers, at law or otherwise. It requires us to confront the most basic of human concerns—the mortality of self and loved ones—*and to balance the interest in preserving human life against the desire to die peacefully and with dignity.* [My emphasis.]

While the case does raise an "extraordinarily important issue" of whether only *terminally* ill Americans have an unqualified right to die, it is not a "difficult" issue. The Fourteenth Amendment guarantees "liberty" and there is no liberty more fundamental than owning one's life and, as a corollary, disposing of it as one wishes. Without that liberty, nothing else matters.[42]

Moreover, the *en banc* majority made a double error within a single sentence. First, whatever the outcome, the court relied on the same "balancing" analysis that has plagued "rights" adjudication by all American courts seemingly forever. Not only is "balancing" life versus death immoral, but it is a useless exercise, especially when it is applied to a terminal individual's life and death.

> People of good will can and do passionately disagree about the proper result, perhaps even more intensely than they part ways over the constitutionality of restricting a woman's right to have an abortion. Heated though the debate may be, *we must determine whether and how the United States Constitution applies to the controversy before us*, a controversy that may touch more people more profoundly than any other issue the courts will face in the foreseeable future. [My emphasis.]

> Today, we are required to decide whether a person who is *terminally* ill has a constitutionally protected liberty interest in hastening what might otherwise be a protracted, undignified, and extremely painful death. [My emphasis.]

Recall that the limitation imposed by the plaintiffs themselves—framing the only issue the court was empowered to decide—was not whether *every* American can fully control his or her own death, but whether only *terminally ill* Americans could.")

> If such an interest exists, we must next decide whether or not the State of Washington may constitutionally restrict its exercise by banning a form of medical assistance that is frequently requested by terminally ill people who wish to die.

Okay, such an interest does exist.

> We first conclude that *there is a constitutionally protected liberty interest in determining the time and manner of one's own death.* [My emphasis.]

An interest that is absolute, one that cannot be trumped?

Of course not. It is:

> *an interest that must be weighed against the state's legitimate and countervailing interests, especially those that relate to the preservation of human life.* [My emphasis.]

So, with the judiciary weighing the scales, it is the interests of the death-seekers against the interests of the non-death seekers. (What happens when the scale weighs differently, we shall soon see.)

The moral and constitutionally protected "right" to die exists, then, after judges weigh the value of controlling one's death against what interests others have in the would-be suicide continuing to live and suffer. That is neither a moral nor constitutional "right." It is judicial seven-card stud, with the sufferer as the pot.

> After balancing the competing interests, we conclude by answering the narrow question before us: *We hold that insofar as the Washington statute prohibits physicians from prescribing life-ending medication for use by terminally ill, competent adults who wish to hasten their own deaths, it violates the Due Process* [liberty] *Clause of the Fourteenth Amendment.* [My emphasis.]

All well and good. But it is important to understand that the so-called "right" of self-termination is merely a gift from government, not the exercise of a moral or authentic constitutional right.

In doing its balancing act, what scale did the court use to weigh the individual's right to die against the destructive principles of altruism, collectivism, and statism?

Said the court:

> *There is no litmus test for courts to apply when deciding whether or not a liberty interest exists under the Due Process Clause. Our decisions* involve difficult judgments regarding the *conscience, traditions, and fundamental tenets of our nation.* We must sometimes apply those basic principles in light of *changing values based on shared experience.* Other times we must apply them to *new problems* arising out of the development and use of *new technologies.* In all cases, our analysis of the applicability of the protections of the Constitution must be made in light of *existing circumstances as well as our historic traditions.* [My emphasis.]

Not only does this sound familiar (see the previous chapters), but once again a court invoked Living Constitutionalism. The Ninth Circuit majority—*which reached the right conclusion, but by going down the wrong road*—incanted "ordered liberty," "traditions of our people," and such, and resurrected the usual suspects, our friends from previous chapters: *Palko, Moore, Poe, Griswold, Roe, Casey*, and some of the others, all brought to us by the magic of *substantive* due process and the incorporation doctrine.

The three dissenters balanced the moral and constitutional right to die against the state's time-worn alleged interests of why government, society, altruists, collectivists, statists, voters, and neighbors had so much weight to put on the scales. Thus, the three dissenters apparently had no problem with those suffering physical pain, and those whose selves had retreated into the empty and terror-filed world of lost cognition, left to suffer in their beds and wish—nay, beg—that the Supreme Court of the United States would release them with the blessing of death from their pain or unawareness of the life around them.

Sadly, it was not to be!

13.

WASHINGTON V. GLUCKSBERG: SUPREME COURT OF THE UNITED STATES

The foundation of *Washington* v. *Glucksberg* was built on decades of indefensible Supreme Court decisions that rewrote the Constitution and made inevitable and predictable the outcome of the right-to-die case. To reiterate:

- Procedural due process had morphed into substantive due process.

- Via the Fourteenth Amendment, despite the Tenth Amendment's reservation of powers to the states virtually the entire federal Bill of Rights had been incorporated into prohibitions on state legislation.

- Woolly tests such as "justice," "reasonable," "traditional," "history," and "ordered liberty" were used to substantively evaluate the constitutionality of such legislation.

- The destruction of Tenth Amendment-guaranteed state police power—health, safety, welfare, and morals—rested on such slogans and others such as "penumbras" and "emanations."

- The norm became that state and federal government has a

role in every aspect of its citizens' lives, including life and especially death.

- The constitutionally mandated core principles of federalism, separation of powers, and judicial review were abnegated and replaced by administrative agencies, a parallel government possessing executive, legislative, and judicial power.

- Often explicitly, recognition that the root and branch of what corrupted the Founders' vision has been what Ayn Rand called "America's 'Inner Contradiction'"— the immoral poison of altruism, collectivism, and statism.

In the Introduction to his article "*Washington* v. *Glucksberg* Was Tragically Wrong,"[43] Professor Erwin Chemerinsky has written:

> Properly focused, there were two questions before the Supreme Court in Washington v. Glucksberg. First, in light of all the other non-textual rights protected under the "liberty" of the [federal] Due Process Clause, is the right to assisted death a fundamental right? Second, if so, is the prohibition of assisted death necessary to achieve a compelling [government] interest? Presented in this way, it is clear that the Court erred in Washington v. Glucksberg. The right of a *terminally* ill person to end his or her life is an essential aspect of autonomy, comparable to aspects of autonomy that the Court has protected in decisions concerning *family* autonomy, *reproductive* autonomy, and autonomy to engage in *sexual activity*. Moreover, the *government's interest in protecting* life and preventing suicide has far less force when applied to a *terminally ill* patient. The tragedy of Washington v. Glucksberg is that every day across the country, *terminally* ill patients are being forced to suffer longer and being denied an essential aspect of their autonomy and personhood. [My emphasis.]

I agree with Professor Chemerinsky that the pain of terminal patients must be alleviated and that their choice of when, where, why, and how to die must be respected and protected. However, I disagree that such choice should be limited to the terminally ill, and that substantive due process is the route to get there.

Sadly, Professor Chemerinsky accepts, at least for the purpose of his article, the magical conversion of procedural to substantive due process; the use of every substantive due process test; the incorporation doctrine; a Living Constitution; the proposition that government has a prominent role in virtually every aspect of its citizens' lives; and the consequences to our Republic of the foregoing. More importantly, in doing so, he fails to address what has betrayed the Founding, what Ayn Rand has called altruism, collectivism, and statism.

My argument is different. It is that *Americans do not own our lives and do not control our deaths because the core of the "right-to-die" prohibition is those three immoral, unconstitutional, indefensible, and destructive doctrines.*

Lest there be any doubt that these three "isms" infuse the unanimous Supreme Court's *Glucksberg* decision, explain government control of every American's life and death, condemn uncountable numbers of individuals and their loved ones to avoidable pain and suffering, and drive *Glucksberg's* result, one need focus only on the majority opinion.

- In the State of Washington, "it has *always* been a crime to assist a suicide."

- "We begin, as we do in all due process cases, by examining our Nation's *history, legal traditions, and practices.*"

- Anti-suicide laws "are *longstanding expressions* of the State's commitment to the protection and preservation of all human life."

- For over 700 years, the Anglo-American common-law

tradition has punished or otherwise disapproved of both suicide and assisting suicide.

- Suicide is a *public wrong*.
- Suicide could impact negatively on the sufferer's *family*.
- Anti-suicide laws are acceptable because "the States are currently engaged in serious, *thoughtful examinations* of physician assisted suicide and other similar issues." [My emphasis.]

Justice Stevens concurred [All following italics are my emphasis.]:

- The State has an "*unqualified interest* in the *preservation* of human life.
- "The State has an interest in preserving and fostering the benefits that every human being may provide to the *community. The value to others of a person's life is far too precious to allow the individual to claim a constitutional entitlement to complete autonomy in making a decision to end that life.*"
- "[A]s a general matter the State's interest in the *contributions each person may make to society*... ." [My emphasis.]

Justice Souter also concurred.

In *Glucksberg*, the challenge to Washington's anti-suicide law was based on "substantive" due process. So, consider the following, quoted favorably by Justice Souter from Justice Harlan's dissent in *Poe v. Ullman*:

Due Process has *not been reduced to any formula*; its *content cannot be determined* by reference to any code. The best that can be said is that through the course of this Court's decisions it has represented the *balance* which our Nation, built upon postulates of respect for the liberty of the individual has struck *between that liberty and the demands of organized society.* * * * The balance of which I speak is the balance struck by this country, having regard to what *history* teaches are the traditions from which it developed as well as the traditions from which it broke. *That tradition is a living thing.* [My emphasis.]

Thus, because anti-suicide laws have always existed in our nation's history, legal traditions, and practices for over 700 years, because such laws are currently undergoing thoughtful examination in various states which are laboratories to test democratically generated legislation, because suicide is a public wrong which might punish the suffering patient's family and others, and because individuals who commit suicide can no longer contribute to the community, human life must be preserved by the state no matter at what costs to the sufferers and their loved ones.

Who are the winners and losers in that choice?

What about the interests of the individual who wants to die?

In this regard, consider the hypocrisy of the long history of capital punishment; exoneration for killing in self-defense; the legality of a healthy patient refusing medical treatment even it means death; uncountable American draftees killed in every war, police action, skirmishes, even during peacetime, and beginning with the Civil War; the immoral contradiction of a pregnant woman legally killing her baby but committing a felony if she assists another human being to die.

These are some examples of the government's "unqualified interest" in the preservation of human life." With that kind of "unqualified interest," we don't need disinterest.

14.

NINTH AMENDMENT AND UNENUMERATED RIGHTS

On September 17, 1787, the new Constitution of the United States of America was signed by 38 of the 41 delegates present. Approval by nine of the thirteen states was necessary for ratification.

Even though nowhere in the Constitution were individual rights being surrendered—only power delegated to, and withheld from, the new federal government—opposition to the Constitution was fierce. Fear of a strong central government coupled with the absence of explicit guarantees of individual rights gave pause to many Americans who had broken with England in the name of life, liberty, individual rights, and limited government—and independence.

Recall *Federalist 84*, where Alexander Hamilton acknowledged the problem:

> It has been several times truly remarked that bills of rights are, in their origin, stipulations between kings and their subjects, abridgements of prerogative in favor of privilege, reservations of rights not surrendered to the prince. Such was Magna Charta obtained by the barons, sword in hand, from King John.

The barons were subjects of the king, therefore mere supplicants seeking *privileges*, such as "due process of law." Americans, however, were free men and women, *entitled* to life, liberty, property, individual rights, limited government, and the pursuit of happiness *as a matter of natural right.*

Hamilton continued:

> It is evident, therefore, that, according to their primitive signification, they have no application to Constitutions, professedly founded upon the power of the people, and executed by their immediate representatives and servants. Here, in strictness, the people surrender nothing [i.e., their rights]; and as they retain every thing [i.e., their rights] they have no need of particular reservations. "We, the People of the United States, to secure the blessings of liberty to ourselves and our posterity, do *ordain* and *establish* this constitution for the United States of America. [Emphasis in original.]

> Here is a better recognition of popular rights than volumes of the aphorisms which make the principal figure in several of our state bill of rights, and which would sound much better in a treatise of ethics than in the constitution of government. [Emphasis in original.]

In other words, the Constitution's genesis—unlike monarchical power, supposedly a gift from God to kings and queens, who may or may not grant dispensations such as due process of law—is in the people, and it is they through their Constitution who create and define the limits of government.

Then, consummate lawyer Alexander Hamilton reinforced his argument:

> I go further, and affirm that bills of rights, in the sense and to the extent in which they are contended for, are not only unnecessary in the proposed Constitution, but would even be *dangerous*. They would contain various

exceptions to powers not granted; and, on this very account, would afford a colorable pretext to claim more than were granted. *For why declare that things shall not be done which there is no power to do?* Why, for instance, should it be said that the liberty of the press shall not be restrained, when no power is given by which restrictions may be imposed? I will not contend that such a provision would confer a regulating power; but it is evident that it would furnish, to men disposed to usurp, a plausible pretense for claiming that power. They might urge with a semblance of reason, that the Constitution ought not to be charged with the absurdity of providing against the abuse of an authority which was not given, and that the provision against restraining the liberty of the press afforded a clear implication, that a power to prescribe proper regulations concerning it was intended to be vested in the national government. [My emphasis.]

In other words, do not make a list of rights because whatever is omitted could arguably not exist.

Hamilton won. The Constitution was ratified without a bill of rights.

The first Congress met in March 1789.

James Madison introduced ten amendments designed to protect the individual rights of the American people against violation by the *federal* government: "*Congress* shall make no law... ." [My emphasis.]

Several years later, the Supreme Court would note that Madison's purpose was "to quiet the apprehension of many that without some such declaration of rights, the government would assume and might be held to possess the power to trespass upon those rights of persons and property which by the Declaration of Independence were affirmed to be unalienable rights."[44]

Had Madison, another brilliant lawyer, forgotten about his *Federalist* co-author's argument about the danger of a bill of rights?

Hardly. He had a perfect answer to Hamilton:

> It has been objected also against a bill of rights, that, by enumerating particular exceptions to the grant of power, it would disparage those rights which were not placed in that enumeration, and it might follow by implication, that those rights which were not singled out, were intended to be assigned into the hands of the general government, and were consequently insecure. *This is one of the most plausible arguments I have ever heard urged against the admission of a bill of rights into this system; but I conceive, that may be guarded against. I have attempted it.* [My emphasis.]

> *The enumeration in the Constitution, of certain rights, shall not be construed to deny or disparage others retained by the people. (Amendment IX, Constitution of the United States of America.)*

We know what the Ninth Amendment's reference to *enumerated* rights is in the Constitution: Amendments I through VIII. But what are the *unenumerated* rights of Amendment IX?

If the answer to this question depends on finding a Supreme Court case whose outcome protecting an individual right rests squarely on a specific Amendment IX *unenumerated* right, the research will come to naught. While a Westlaw search of "Ninth Amendment" produces thirty-seven case mentions, *in not one of them did the result rest squarely on the Ninth Amendment.*

Indeed, in Justice Souter's lengthy *Glucksberg* concurring opinion he does not once mention the Ninth Amendment. Not once. Instead, he skirts the issue by talking about "unenumerated" rights.

What are they?

As examples of *his* understanding, Souter cites three Supreme Court cases—*Planned Parenthood v. Casey*,[45] *Poe v. Ullman, and Griswold v. Connecticut*—"comprising a continuum of rights to be free from 'arbitrary impositions and purposeless restraints.'"

According to Justice Souter, the rulings in those cases were rooted in the Court's belief that there were "certain interests requir[ing] particularly careful scrutiny of the State needs asserted to justify their abridgment."

In support of that proposition, he cited two additional cases—*Skinner v. Oklahoma*[46] and *Corfield v. Coryell*[47]—"that is, interests in liberty sufficiently important to be judged 'fundamental.' In the face of an interest this powerful a State may not rest on threshold rationality or a presumption of constitutionality but may prevail only on the ground of an interest *sufficiently compelling* to place within the realm of the reasonable a refusal to recognize the individual right asserted." [My emphasis.]

So, let's examine the *raison d'être*—defined in Websters as "the most important reason or purpose for someone or something's existence"—for why the interests in these five cases were so important as to be deemed unenumerated yet fundamental.

Corfield, an irrelevant case decided by the Supreme Court in 1823, involved a New Jersey law that regulated clam digging. Hardly a "fundamental right."

Skinner held a habitual criminal sterilization law violative of substantive due process. Writing for the majority, Justice Douglas said that the Court "was dealing here with legislation which involves one of the basic civil rights of man" (apparently, Carrie Buck never got the memo). Apparently, not being involuntarily sterilized is more "fundamental" than ending one's life.

Why?

"Because," Douglas said for the Court, "marriage and procreation are fundamental to *the very existence and survival of the race.*

The power to sterilize, if exercised, may have subtle, far reaching and devastating effects. In evil or reckless hands, *it can cause races or types which are inimical to the dominant group to wither and disappear*. Could he have been thinking about eugenics? [My emphasis.]

In concurring, Justice Stone said, "*the State* [lots of people] *may protect itself* from the demonstrably inheritable tendencies of the individual which are *injurious to society* [lots more people]...." [My emphasis.]

As to *Griswold* v. *Connecticut* and *Poe* v. *Ullman* (decided before Roe) and *Planned Parenthood* v. *Casey* (decided after), it was more of the same.

Recall that *Griswold* rested on the existence of emanations and penumbras, and that *Poe* contained a dissent by Justice Harlan, who recognized explicitly that regulation of "*morality [is] among State concerns* [and] indicates that *society* is not limited in its objects only to the physical well-being of the community, but has traditionally concerned itself with *the moral soundness* of its people as well." [My emphasis.]

Harlan continued in *Skinner*:

> Indeed, to attempt a line between public behavior and that which is purely consensual or solitary would be to *withdraw from community concern* a range of subjects with which *every society in civilized times has found it necessary to deal*." [My emphasis.]

By now, it should be clear to the reader that in the Court's and Justice Souter's jurisprudential world, enumerated rights rest not on the nature of Americans or natural rights, but instead on the ephemeral trio of altruism, collectivism, and statism.

That said, it is fitting to end Justice Souter's case citations in *Glucksberg* with a quotation from *Roe* v. *Wade*:

> Roe, a pregnant woman, *cannot be isolated* in her privacy.

She carries an embryo and, later, a fetus ... The situation therefore is inherently different from marital intimacy, or bedroom possession of obscene material, or marriage, or procreation, or education, with which [other cases] ... were respectively concerned. As we have intimated above, *it is reasonable and appropriate for a State to decide that at some point in time another interest, that of health of the mother or that of potential human life, becomes significantly involved.* The woman's privacy is no longer sole and any right of privacy she possesses must be measured accordingly. [My emphasis.]

The state—which is "society," which is other people—has an interest in Ms. Roe and her unborn baby, so much so that a mother could have (and did) kill that child with impunity on the Supreme Court's original *Roe* trimester schedule and later using its "viability" standard. Just as the State of Oregon had an interest in the well-being of Emma Gotcher, whose livelihood it destroyed. Just as the State of Virginia had an interest in the involuntary sterilization of Carrie Buck. After all, as Justice Holmes wrote for the 8-1 *Buck* Court, "Three generations of imbeciles are enough."

For whom?[48]

15.

CONCLUSION

In *Planned Parenthood* v. *Casey*, ignoring his and the majority's shameful hypocrisy and providing the consummate example of the altruism, collectivism, and statism that has pervaded American jurisprudence from the beginning—which Ayn Rand called America's "inner contradiction"—Justice Kennedy wrote:

> Our law affords constitutional protection to personal decisions relating to marriage, procreation, contraception, family relationships, child rearing, and education [because a due process analysis considers them "fundamental rights] * * * Our cases recognize "the right of the *individual,* married or single, to be *free from unwarranted governmental intrusion* into matters so *fundamentally affecting* a person as the decision whether to *bear or beget a child." * * *
>
> Our precedents "have respected the private realm of family life which the State cannot enter. These matters, *involving the most intimate and personal* choices a person may make in a *lifetime,* choices central to personal dignity and autonomy, are central to the liberty protected by the Fourteenth Amendment. *At the heart of liberty is the right to define one's own concept of existence*, of meaning, of the universe, and of the mystery of human

life. Beliefs about these matters could not define the attributes of personhood were they formed under compulsion of the State." [Bracketed words and emphasis are mine.]

Justice Kennedy's sentence—"At the heart of liberty *is* the right to define one's own concept of existence"—needs to be corrected because it is a lie. *No such right exists, thanks to the Supreme Court of the United States.* [My emphasis.]

If this is a free country and would remain one, the sentence needs to say, "At the heart of liberty *must* be the right to define one's own concept of existence."

Why?

Because in today's America the choice of life or death (*Roe, Casey, Glucksberg*) *is* definitely "formed under compulsion of the State" and will continue to be until the altruists, collectivists, and statists are no longer allowed to "define ... [the individual's] own concept of existence."

And, most important, the individual's own concept of *non-existence*.[49]

ENDNOTES

1 *Webster's* defines "eugenics" as "the movement devoted to improving through the human species through the control of hereditary factors in mating." This definition does not note that the "movement" employed forced male and female sterilization for "improvement." Later, for "improvement," the Nazis employed murder.

2 The "undesirable" class included Negroes.

3 571 U.S. 702 (1997). All the justices' opinions combined totaled more than one hundred pages.

4 The eleven state "assisted suicide" statutes appear to make an effort not to use the word "suicide."

5 In 2005, Robert H. Bork, former Yale law professor, judge of the United States Court of Appeals for the District of Columbia Circuit, and cruelly defeated nominee for a seat on the Supreme Court of the United States, observed:

For the past 20 years, conservatives have been articulating the philosophy of originalism, the only approach that can make judicial review democratically legitimate. Originalism simply means that the judge must discern from the relevant materials—debates at the Constitutional Convention, the Federalist Papers and Anti-Federalist Papers, newspaper accounts of the time, debates in the State ratifying conventions, and the like—*the principles the ratifiers understood themselves to be enacting.* The remainder of the task is to apply those principles to unforeseen circumstances, a task that law performs all the time. *Any philosophy that does not confine judges to the original understanding inevitably makes the Constitution the plaything of willful judges.* [My emphasis.]

6   Declaration of Independence. July 4, 1776.

7   *Ibid.*

8   The reference to the first ten amendments as the "Bill of Rights" (1787) is a misnomer. The Tenth Amendment provides: "The powers not delegated to the United States by the Constitution, nor prohibited by it to the States, are reserved to the States respectively, or to the people." [My emphasis.]

9   7 Pet. 243 (1833).

10 547 U.S. 220 (2006). I quote Justice Thomas often and at length because currently he is the Supreme Court's leading originalist and is clear and correct about important subjects of constitutional law, especially individual rights and limited government.

11 2 U.S. (2 Dall.) 304 (1795).

12 13 N.Y. 378 (1856).

13 60 U.S. (19 How.) 393 (1857).

14 44 *Brooklyn Law Review* 725 (1978).

15 96 U.S. 97 (1878)

16 123 U.S. 623 (1887).

17 134 U.S. 418 (1890).

18 171 U.S. 362 (1898).

19 218 U.S. 412 (1908).

20 A "starcher" was the term used in those days by the laundry industry for the employee whose job it was to apply starch to dress shirts. In the early 1900s, rarely were hand laundries firmly instructed, "No starch."

21 Emma's father's employer did give the Gotcher family only

a lump of coal for Christmas. Tiny Tim did not get his sled for Christmas.

22 This is the same rationale that underlay the monstrous program that would exist a quarter-century later in Nazi Germany.

23 268 U.S. 652 (1925).

24 249 U.S. 47 (1919).

25 302 U.S. 319 (1937).

26 395 U.S. 784 (1969).

27 See below, *Poe* v. *Ullman*, *Griswold* v. *Connecticut*, *Roe* v. *Wade*, and *Planned Parenthood* v. *Casey*.

28 *Timbs* v. *Indiana*, 586 U.S.___, 139 S.Ct. 682 (2019).

29 Some citations in Justice Thomas's opinion are omitted throughout.

30 367 U.S. 497 (1956).

31 381 U.S. 479 (1965).

32 The intent and wording of the statute included heterosexual married couples.

33 In *Griswold*, the *federal* Supreme *Court* was deciding the constitutionality of a *state legislative/executive* enactment.

34 *Webster's New World Dictionary of the American Language* defines "penumbra" as the "partly lighted area surrounding the complete shadow of a body, as the moon, in full eclipse ... the less dark region surrounding the dark central area of a sunspot ... a vague, indefinite, or borderline area."

35 *Webster's* defines "emanation" as "to flow out, arise ... come forth ... issue ... as from a source."

36 Note Harlan lumping together adultery (at least one party married), homosexuality (same gender), and fornication (consensual, presumably adult) on the one hand, and incest (sibling and other familial relationships) on the other. The first three are quite different from the fourth.

37 410 U.S. 113 (1973).

38 432 U.S. 464 (1977).

39 49 F.3d 586(1995).

40 497 U.S. 261 (1990).

41 A *reductio ad absurdum* is a method of trying to prove that a premise or stated proposition is false or unworkable by showing that its logical consequence is absurd or contradictory.

42 Ayn Rand has written that "There is only one fundamental alternative in the Universe: existence or nonexistence," meaning life or death.

43 106 *Mich. L. Rev.* 1501 (2008).

44 148 U.S. 312 (1893).

45 505 U.S. 833 (1992).

46 316 U.S. 535 (1942).

47 6 F.Cas. 546 (1823).

48 For additional information about Carrie Buck and *Buck* v. *Bell*, see Jennifer Senior's March 6, 2016, *New York Times* review, *Imbeciles on the Supreme Court* and *Justice Not for All* by Adam Cohen. The following quotations are from Ms. Senior's review. [Bracketed words are mine].

Ms. Buck was neither epileptic nor feebleminded. As time would prove, she was of perfectly average intelligence. She was simply uneducated and luckless—a poor white girl from

Charlottesville who'd had a baby at 17, most likely because she'd been raped by the nephew of her foster mother. Rather than risking scandal, her guardians thought it best to get rid of her.

Nor was Ms. Buck part of three generations of so-called imbeciles.

Of all the tools to stem the tide of feeblemindedness, sterilization was by far the most efficient. During the Progressive Era, a number of states had enacted compulsory sterilization laws, including California and Connecticut. So bullish was Dr. Priddy to do the same for Virginia that he worked in concert with a methodical, meticulous local lawmaker, Aubrey Strode, to design a statute that would withstand the test of the highest court of the land. Ms. Buck was the test case.

We learn early on that Ms. Buck's lawyer, Irving Whitehead, had close personal and professional ties to the Virginia Colony for Epileptics and Feeble-Minded—the superintendent paid his legal fees—which meant he [the lawyer] made no efforts to mount a serious defense for his client.

Justice Holmes [was] himself an eager eugenicist.

49 505 U.S. 833 (1992).

50 "Health Care Provider"—an individual who can be involved in the acts described above—as "a physician licensed pursuant to the Medical Practice Act; an osteopathic physician licensed pursuant to the Osteopathic Medicine Act; a nurse licensed in advanced practice pursuing to the Nursing Practice Act; or a physician assistant licensed pursuant to the Physician Assistant Act or the Osteopathic Medicine Act.

APPENDIX A

As of this writing, the following are the eleven states that have created an alleged means for their citizens to a "right to die."

To date, three methods have been used: Ballot initiatives (3) legislation (7), and judicial opinion (1).

California

Bill Text - SB-380 End of life. (ca.gov)

Colorado

Colorado Legal Resources (lexis.com)

District of Colombia

Death With Dignity Act.FINAL.pdf (dc.gov)

Hawaii

OCOC-Act2.pdf (hawaii.gov)

Maine

HP0948, LD 1313, item 1, An Act To Enact the Maine Death with Dignity Act (mainelegislature.org)

Montana

Baxter v Montana (law.justia.com)

New Jersey

Medical-Aid-in-Dying-for-the-Terminally-Ill-Act.pdf (njconsumeraffairs.gov)

New Mexico

CH132-HB47-2021.pdf (endoflifeoptionsnm.org)

Oregon

statute.pdf (oregon.gov)

Vermont

No. 39. An act relating to patient choice and control at end of life (state.vt.us)

Washington State

The Washington Death With Dignity Act (apps.leg.wa.gov)

APPENDIX B

It is noteworthy that in *Glucksberg* the Supreme Court mentioned that "Respondents [plaintiffs in the federal district court] fully embrace the notion that the State must be free to impose reasonable regulations on physician assistance *to assure that the patients they assist are competent and terminally ill and that each has made a free and informed choice in seeking to obtain and use a fatal drug.*" [My emphasis.]

In fact, the statutes, rules, practices and "reasonable regulations" governing the so-called "right-to-die" in the states listed above are mostly a cruel sham and expose the heavy hand of the state.

The government intrusion into the most personal act an individual can perform, committing suicide, is so onerous that satisfying its conditions are extremely difficult. Often, complying with all the requirements comes too late to spare the terminal patient needless pain, let alone loss of cognitive capacity, while his or her loved ones stand by helplessly.

As proof, I offer selected examples from New Mexico's "End-of-Life Options Act," the most recent such statute in the nation.

While enactment effective June 18, 2021, has been hailed in New Mexico and elsewhere as a major advancement in recognizing an individual's right to determine the when, where, why, and how of his or her death, the new law not only falls far short, but almost seems deliberately to create impediments.

Required by a core requirement of the Act in Section 2J is that the patient must be terminally ill, statutorily defined as having "a *disease* or *condition* that is *incurable* and *irreversible* and that, in accordance with *reasonable* medical judgment, *will* result in death within *six* months."

These four requirements are an invitation to litigation, with judges or possibly juries asked to define each of the italicized words to ascertain whether the patient is "terminal and thus satisfies the statutory definitional requirement."

Because the Act is new, judges in New Mexico, especially the State Supreme Court, must turn for guidance to case law in other states which allow physician-assisted death.

The Act's impact on the patient's physician is so onerous, rather than attempt to paraphrase it, the statute can speak for itself:

> A prescribing health care provider may provide a prescription for medical aid in dying medication to an individual only after the prescribing health care provider has:
>
>> A. determined that the individual has:
>>
>>> (1.) capacity;
>>>
>>> (2.) a terminal illness;
>>>
>>> (3.) voluntarily made the request for medical aid in dying; and
>>>
>>> (4.) the ability to self-administer the medical aid in dying medication;
>>
>> B. provided medical care to the individual in accordance with accepted medical standards of care;
>>
>> C. determined that the individual is making an informed decision after discussing with the individual the:

(1.) individual's medical diagnosis and prognosis;

(2.) potential risks associated with self-administering the medical aid in dying medication that the individual has requested the health care provider to prescribe;

(3.) probable result of self-administering the medical aid in dying medication to be prescribed;

(4.) individual's option of choosing to obtain the medical aid in dying medication and then deciding not to use it; and

(5.) feasible alternative, concurrent or additional treatment opportunities, including hospice care and palliative care focused on relieving symptoms and reducing suffering;

D. determined in good faith that the individual's request does not arise from coercion or undue influence by another person;

E. noted in the individual's health record the prescribing health care provider's determination that the individual qualifies to receive medical aid in dying;

F. confirmed in the individual's health record that at least one physician or osteopathic physician licensed pursuant to the Medical Practice Act or the Osteopathic Medicine Act has determined, after conducting an appropriate examination, that the individual has capacity, a terminal illness and the ability to self-administer the medical aid in dying medication. That physician may be the prescribing health care provider pursuant to this section, the individual's hospice health care provider or another physician who meets the requirements of this subsection;

G. affirmed that the individual is:

   (1.) enrolled in a medicare-certified hospice program; or

   (2.) eligible to receive medical aid in dying after the prescribing health care provider has referred the individual to a consulting health care provider, who has experience with the underlying condition rendering the qualified individual terminally ill, and the consulting health care provider has:

   (a.) examined the individual;

   (b.) reviewed the individual's relevant medical records; and

   (c.) confirmed, in writing, the prescribing health care provider's prognosis that the individual is suffering from a terminal illness; and

H. provided substantially the following form to the individual and enters the form into the individual's health record after the form has been completed with all of the required signatures and initials:

"REQUEST FOR MEDICATION TO END MY LIFE IN A PEACEFUL MANNER

I, _____, am an adult of sound mind.

I am suffering from a terminal illness, which is a disease or condition that is incurable and irreversible and that, according to reasonable medical judgment, will result in my death within six months. My health care provider has determined that the illness is in its terminal phase.

Appendix B

_____

(Patient Initials)

I have been fully informed of my diagnosis and prognosis, the nature of the medical aid in dying medication to be prescribed and the potential associated risks, the expected result and the feasible alternative, concurrent or additional treatment opportunities, including hospice care and palliative care focused on relieving symptoms and reducing suffering.

_____

(Patient Initials)

I request that my health care provider prescribe medication that will end my life in a peaceful manner if I choose to self-administer the medication, and I authorize my health care provider to contact a willing pharmacist to fulfill this request.

_____

(Patient Initials)

I understand that I have the right to rescind this request at any time.

_____

(Patient Initials)

I understand the full import of this request, and I expect to die if I self-administer the medical aid in dying medication prescribed. I further understand that although most deaths occur within three hours, my death may take longer. My health care provider has counseled me about this possibility.

_____

(Patient Initials)

I make this request voluntarily and without reservation.

Signed: _____

Date: _____

Time: _____

DECLARATION OF WITNESSES:

We declare that the person signing this request:

> A. is personally known to us or has provided proof of identity;
>
> B. signed this request in our presence;
>
> C. appears to be of sound mind and not under duress, fraud or undue influence; and
>
> D. is not a patient for whom either of us is a health care provider.

Witness 1 _____

Printed Name: _____

Relationship to Patient: _____

Date: _____

Witness 2 _____

Printed Name: _____

Relationship to Patient: _____

Date: _____

NOTE: No more than one witness shall be a relative by blood, marriage or adoption of the person signing this request. No more than one witness shall own, operate or be employed at a health care facility where the person signing this request is a patient or resident.".

As if the burden on the patient's own physician is not enough, he or she must find another qualified physician willing to assume the burden spelled out in paragraph F above.

There's more in the act: Informing the patient of other options; who is immune for what; conscience-based decisions; prohibited acts; reporting requirements; how to determine capacity; waiting periods.

That's a tall order for someone who is terminal and facing death within six months, let alone for his physicians and caretakers.

When considering the meta-onerousness of attempting to comply with New Mexico's End-of-life options act, one wonders how many statutory "Health Care Providers"[50] – especially Nurses and Physician Assistants – will be willing to be intimately involved in another person's death.

Hoops, hurdles, obstacles, barriers, impediments, and difficulties … all to assist and die a peaceful death.

OTHER BOOKS BY HENRY MARK HOLZER

FICTION

A Fool for a Client?

The Paladin Curse (Co-author with Erika Holzer)

NON FICTION

The American Constitution and Ayn Rand's "Inner Contradiction"

Best Opinions of the Supreme Court of the United States (Vol. I: Race) (E-Book)

The Supreme Court Opinions of Clarence Thomas, 1991–2011 (Second Edition)

The Supreme Court Opinions of Clarence Thomas, 1991–2006 (First Edition)

The Keeper of the Flame

"Aid and Comfort": Jane Fonda in North Vietnam (with Erika Holzer)

Fake Warriors: Identifying, Exposing, and Punishing Those Who Falsify Their Military Service (with Erika Holzer) *(Second Edition)*

Fake Warriors: Identifying, Exposing, and Punishing: Those Who Falsify Their Military Service (with Erika Holzer) *(First Edition)*

Why Not Call It Treason? Korea, Vietnam, Afghanistan and Today

The Layman's Guide to Tax Evasion

Speaking Freely: The Case Against Speech Codes (ed.)

Sweet Land of Liberty? The Supreme Court and Individual Rights

Government's Money Monopoly: Its Origin and Scope and How to Fight It (ed.)

The Gold Clause: What it is and how to use it profitably (ed.)

ACKNOWLEDGMENTS

PB and EY in California and AT in New Mexico know why I am grateful. This book is silently dedicated to them.

Understandably, after the Supreme Court's decision in *Glucksberg v. Washington*, individuals and entities in the Right-to-Die Movement seem to have given up on litigation as a means of fighting another round in the Right-to-Die War (which is there for the taking). Nevertheless, despite my critical comments above about the plaintiffs' moral and tactical concession in *Glucksberg*, the Movement deserves thanks for the litigation they brought and the legislative battles they have fought.

My new copy editor, Stephen England, has the eyes of an Eagle and is an accomplished thriller author in his own right.

Also thanks to Robert Bidinotto and Streetlight Graphics for help with publishing this book.

HENRY MARK HOLZER

Henry Mark Holzer received his B.A. degree from New York University, where he studied political science and Russian. After graduation in 1954, he served in South Korea with United States Army intelligence (G-2), holding top-secret security clearance, and was Chief Order of Battle Analyst (Chinese Communist Forces), attached to Eighth Army Headquarters in Seoul.

Following Holzer's military service, he earned his Juris Doctor degree at New York University School of Law. For some sixty years, he practiced constitutional and appellate law. His clients included owners of pre-legalized gold, veterans seeking medical benefits, Soviet dissidents and defectors, and the author Ayn Rand.

In addition to Henry Mark Holzer's law practice, for two decades (1972-1993) he was a full-time professor of law at Brooklyn Law School, where he is now professor emeritus. His courses included Constitutional Law, First Amendment, National Security, and Appellate Advocacy. He spent one semester as a visiting professor at the University of New Mexico School of Law in 1993.

Professor Holzer is the author of hundreds of articles, essays, and reviews, and for many years he frequently published commentary on current legal/political issues and events in the print and electronic media. He was often invited to provide that commentary on broadcast media.

Several of Professor Holzer's six out-of-print books—*The Gold Clause*; *Government's Money Monopoly*; *Sweet Land* of Liberty? The Supreme Court and Individual Rights; The Layman's Guide to Tax Evasion; Speaking Freely: The Case Against Speech Codes; and Why Not Call It Treason? Korea, Vietnam, Afghanistan and Today—may be available through his website, www.henrymarkholzer.com and from various Internet booksellers, including www.amazon.com.

With lawyer and novelist Erika Holzer, Henry Mark Holzer is co-author of "Aid and Comfort": Jane Fonda in North Vietnam, the seminal book that definitively answers the question of whether Fonda's trip to Hanoi during the Vietnam War, and her activities there, constituted constitutional treason. With Erika Holzer, Professor Holzer also co-authored Fake Warriors: Identifying, Exposing, and Punishing Those Who Falsify Their Military Service. Some of these books may be available through his website, www.henrymarkholzer.com, and all are from various Internet booksellers, including www.amazon.com.

Professor Holzer's The Supreme Court Opinions of Justice Clarence Thomas (1991–2011): A Conservative's Perspective, second edition, was published in 2012. McFarland and Company is a noted publisher of scholarly, reference, and academic books. See https://www.abebooks.com/9780786463343/Supreme-Court-Opinions-Clarence-Thomas-0786463341/plp

His most recent non-fiction book is The American Constitution and Ayn Rand's "Inner Contradiction."

Professor Holzer previously blogged at www.henrymarkholzer.blogspot.com. A selection of his essays appears there.

www.ingramcontent.com/pod-product-compliance
Lightning Source LLC
Chambersburg PA
CBHW031921240526
45464CB00021B/627